TWELVE
PILLARS

With

LIVING WELL, WORKING SMART

Soft Skills for Success

Workbook

Forward Books LLC
15100 SE 38th ST #787
Bellevue • WA • 98006
PH • 425-653-1582
www.forwardbooks.com

Copyright © 2006 by The Mackey Group

All rights reserved. No part of this book may be reproduced, stored in, or introduced into a retrieval system, or transmitted in any form or by any means (electronic, mechanical, photocopying, recording or otherwise) without the prior written permission of the publisher.

10 9 8 7 6 5 4 3 2

Printed in the United States of America

LCCN 2006927733
ISBN 0-9773262-2-5

Technical Consultant: Eileen Casey White, Ed.D.
Editor: Vicki McCown
Cover: Laura Zugzda
Interior Layout: Stephanie Martindale

Contents

Acknowledgement iv

Introduction v

Pillar One 1

Pillar Two 11

Pillar Three 23

Pillar Four 33

Pillar Five 43

Pillar Six 57

Pillar Seven 69

Pillar Eight 79

Pillar Nine 89

Pillar Ten 103

Pillar Eleven 113

Pillar Twelve 125

Acknowledgement

Our gratitude to Jim Rohn, Kyle Wilson, and Chris Widener for their support and commitment to the development of the *Twelve Pillars of Success Workbook*.

Introduction to Twelve Pillars and Living Well, Working Smart:
Soft Skills for Success

Have you ever wondered after reading a great book on how to succeed what the rest of the story is? Or, asked yourself why it's so easy for some but so challenging for others? Or, understood WHAT, you were instructed to do but didn't know HOW to do it and do it successfully? Or, thought if these are the keys to success, why am I not successfully implementing them?

In a first of its kind, the answers are within your workbook. In order to execute the Twelve Pillars, the fundamentals, successfully, you must know which skill sets are required for each and how to use each one effectively. Jim Rohn and Chris Widener, authors of Twelve Pillars, explain what you need to know and do in each Pillar to live a rich and rewarding life. Your workbook identifies the skill sets you will need to know and use with proficiency to make each Pillar work for you. Our book, Living Well, Working Smart: Soft Skills for Success will describe, step by step, how to master each of the skills required to weave a tapestry of Twelve Pillars into your life, for you and your family's future.

What you have before you is unique. Upon completion, your opportunities will be boundless, your rewards immeasurable, your influence unbridled and your legacy worthwhile.

We will be rooting for your success and for all those you mentor along the way!

Pillar One

"The only way things are going to change for you is when you change."

Before you begin this portion of the **Twelve Pillars Workbook**, read or reread Chapter 1, *A Chance Encounter,* of **Twelve Pillars**.

Pillar One

"Mr. Davis has those twelve Pillars of Success I was telling you about. The first one he talks about is Personal Development. Success comes when you develop yourself beyond where you currently are. So you have to work harder on yourself – improving yourself – than you do on your job." (Charlie, **Twelve Pillars***)*

Personal development and self-improvement are an inherent part of our human condition. From birth until death, we face needs and challenges we must meet and overcome. Maturity, confidence, self-esteem, and the ability to contribute are dependent upon our willingness to improve self.

No one is born fully equipped with the knowledge, skills, attitudes, and values required to live a rich and rewarding life; we must seek these attitudes through continual learning and self-improvement. This cycle of personal development begins with the recognition of our strengths and weaknesses and continues with careful examination of their impact on our work, relationships, and overall quality of life. Then, while maintaining our strengths, we must set prioritized goals to address our inefficiencies. Once our goals are established, we must develop the required knowledge and skills to correct or improve our weakest and most problematic areas. Finally, we must honestly assess the outcomes of our efforts, identify residual problems, and repeat the personal development cycle.

As we experience personal improvements, we are often tempted to scrutinize and criticize others for similar faults or weaknesses. Beware: Resist this temptation! It will steal necessary focus from your goals and be resented by others. Personal development is not easy, but it offers personal and professional rewards that are well worth the effort. The following activities will help you reap these rewards.

CRITICAL OUTCOMES FOR PILLAR ONE:
- Identifying Strengths and Weaknesses
- Setting Short-Term Goals

PERSONAL DEVELOPMENT/SELF-IMPROVEMENT

In **Twelve Pillars**, Charlie tells Michael that if he wants to succeed in life, he needs to work harder on himself than he does on his job. The only way things will change is when he changes. Just like Michael, you need to begin by thinking about your strengths and your weaknesses and decide to change what is not working for you. In this activity, reflect on the following skills required to successfully implement personal development/self-improvement and write down your answers to each question.

Skill: Courage

1. What is my clearest and most reliable strength in this skill?

   _____
   _____

2. What do I struggle with the most in this skill?

   _____
   _____

3. How does this struggle or weakness affect my work, my relationships, and the quality of my life?

   _____
   _____

4. How would others describe my strengths and weaknesses in this skill?

   _____
   _____

Skill: Flexibility/Adaptability

1. What is my clearest and most reliable strength in this skill?

   _____
   _____

2. What do I struggle with the most in this skill?

   _____
   _____

3. How does this struggle or weakness affect my work, my relationships, and the quality of my life?

   _____
   _____

4. How would others describe my strengths and weaknesses in this skill?

   _____
   _____

Skill: Optimism/Positive Attitude and Ambition

1. What is my clearest and most reliable strength in this skill?

   _____
   _____

2. What do I struggle with the most in this skill?

   _____
   _____

3. How does this struggle or weakness affect my work, my relationships, and the quality of my life?

   _____
   _____

4. How would others describe my strengths and weaknesses in this skill?

_____
_____

Choose another skill (problem solving, commitment, decision making, etc.) and answer these questions for that skill.

SKILL: _____

1. What is my clearest and most reliable strength in this skill?

   _____
   _____

2. What do I struggle with the most in this skill?

   _____
   _____

3. How does this struggle or weakness affect my work, my relationships, and the quality of my life?

   _____
   _____

4. How would others describe my strengths and weaknesses in this skill?

   _____
   _____

MISTAKES TO AVOID

As you use this workbook, you will find activities that help you focus on developing those skills. You will also have opportunities to reflect on behaviors that may keep you from achieving the level of success for which you strive.

*Which one of these **Mistakes to Avoid** is the one you need to work on changing in your life?*

Skill: Personal Development/Self-Improvement

- **Believing you have reached the pinnacle of perfection with no further need for self-improvement.** Result: Alienate yourself. Be spoken of as self-important, obnoxious, and a fraud.
- **Setting higher standards for others than you set for yourself.** Result: Envy others as they fulfill expectations, rise to the higher standards, and bypass you in their ascent to success.

Skill: Courage

- **Letting past failure or unsubstantiated fears keep you from acting courageously.** Result: Remain trapped by the past and frozen by your fear. Miss the thrill of successfully challenging your fears, moving forward, exploring new possibilities, and embarking on great adventures.
- **Settling for status quo.** Result: Stay in your comfort zone. Envy others for their courage, and complain about your role as a perpetual bystander.

Skill: Flexibility/Adaptability

- **Choosing to see required change as an imposition rather than a possibility.** Result: Insist that the cup is half-empty; refuse to admit that it is also half-full.
- **Refusing to explore different options when faced with the need to change.** Result: Exhibit all the flexibility of a rusted iron gate; ensure that your mental gate remains fixed in place and permanently shut to all possibilities. Throw away the oil can.

Skill: Optimism/Positive Attitude and Ambition

- **Surrounding yourself with negative, depressing, and pessimistic people.** Result: Become like those with whom you associate. Their attitudes infect you like a contagious disease.
- **Maintaining a bad attitude without a desire to improve or contribute to improving conditions or circumstances.** Result: Impart doom and gloom to those around you. Become part of the problem and not part of the solution. Live in a constant state of despair, misery, loneliness, and isolation.

THE MIRACLE OF PERSONAL DEVELOPMENT

In the following article, Jim Rohn (co-author of **Twelve Pillars**) tells the story of how he learned about the importance of Personal Development from his mentor, Mr. Shoaff. Read the short narrative and then answer the reflective questions that follow.

One day Mr. Shoaff said, "Jim, if you want to be wealthy and happy, learn this lesson well: Learn to work harder on yourself than you do on your job."

Since that time I've been working on my own personal development. And I must admit that this has been the most challenging assignment of all. This business of personal development lasts a lifetime.

You see, what you become is far more important than what you get. The important question to ask on the job is not, "What am I getting?" Instead, you should ask, "What am I becoming?" Getting and becoming are like Siamese twins: What you become directly influences what you get. Think of it this way: Most of what you have today you have attracted by becoming the person you are today.

I've also found that income rarely exceeds personal development. Sometimes income takes a lucky jump, but unless you learn to handle the responsibilities that come with it, it will usually shrink back to the amount you can handle.

If someone hands you a million dollars, you'd better hurry up and become a millionaire. A very rich man once said, "If you took all the money in the world and divided it equally among everybody, it would soon be back in the same pockets it was before."

It is hard to keep that which has not been obtained through personal development

So here's the great axiom of life: To Have More Than You've Got, Become More Than You Are.

This is where you should focus most of your attention. Otherwise, you just might have to contend with the axiom of not changing, which is: Unless You Change How You Are, You'll Always Have What You've Got.

(by Jim Rohn)

1. Jim asks, "What are you becoming?" What do you think you want to become?

   _____

   _____

2. Deciding what you want to become is the first step to setting achievable goals for yourself. What is something you can do in the next twenty-four hours that will start you on the path to becoming who you want to be?

_____

_____

3. Short-term goals are tasks that can be achieved in less than six months. They build on your strengths and work to overcome your weaknesses. In the spaces below, write down one of your strengths and one of your weaknesses from the previous section. Think of at least one short-term goal you can set to build on that strength and overcome that weakness. You can't do this alone, so think of who else can support your efforts at succeeding in this Miracle of Personal Development.

Strength: _____

Short-Term Goal to build on it:

_____

_____

Weakness: _____

Short-Term Goal to overcome it:

_____

_____

Name at least one person in your life who can help you evaluate your progress and reach these two goals:

_____

_____

MY LIST OF GOALS

In **Twelve Pillars**, Michael writes down a list of ten things he wants to work on in his life. Reflect on what you have written in the last few pages of this workbook, and in the space below, **write down at least three (but no more than ten) goals, strengths, and/or weaknesses you want to work on in the next month:**

1. _____
2. _____
3. _____
4. _____
5. _____
6. _____
7. _____
8. _____
9. _____
10. _____

Listed below are the Critical Skills needed to be proficient in this Pillar. Also listed are the Additional Essential Skills needed for mastery.

Critical Skills	Additional Essential Skills
Personal Development/Self-Improvement	Problem Solving
Courage	Decision Making
Flexibility/Adaptability	Commitment
Optimism/Positive Attitude and Ambition	Accountability

Pillar Two

"Make sure the outside of you is a good reflection of the inside of you."

Before you begin this portion of the **Twelve Pillars Workbook**, read or reread Chapter 2, *Live a Life of Health,* of **Twelve Pillars**.

Pillar Two

*"Pillar Number Two is Total Well-being. Mr. Davis believes in what he calls Three-dimensional health . . . when you say 'health' to most people, they think of your physical well-being, but Mr. Davis thinks of it as more than that, He thinks that a person is made up of three parts: The body, the soul, and the spirit. Three dimensions." (Charlie, **Twelve Pillars**)*

It's common to hear successful people confirm that success is not one-dimensional. It is, as Mr. Davis explains in this chapter, three-dimensional – or, as we commonly refer to it, achieving balance in our lives. Successful people worth following and emulating are always those who strive to achieve a healthy balance, with dedicated focus on their physical (body) well-being, their soul (mental and emotional), and their spiritual (eternal) well-being. Neglecting one over another is to cheat oneself out of becoming all that one can be and denying the ability to influence others – the joy gained from making a difference in the lives of others.

Using the analogy of an onion, Charlie (**Twelve Pillars**) explains to Michael that the inner core of the onion is our spiritual being, the layer covering the inner core is our soul, and our body is the outer layer. Charlie also speaks of how achieving three-dimensional balance provides us with strength that transfers from one person to another. Think about the people you know who are solid in all three dimensions. You feel their strength, their solidness when in their presence. Peel an onion and you'll discover that, as you get closer to the core, it becomes more difficult to pull away each layer. So, too, is it with those who have Total Well-being.

CRITICAL OUTCOMES FOR PILLAR TWO:
- Identifying three dimensions of personal life
- Setting priorities

IDENTIFY THE THREE DIMENSIONS OF YOUR PERSONAL LIFE

In **Twelve Pillars**, Charlie tells Michael to make sure that the "outside of you is a good reflection of the inside of you." In this activity, use the **Twelve Pillars** book to define each dimension. Then rate yourself on how much you currently focus on developing that dimension in your personal life.

Dimension 1: The Body

Definition:

_____
_____

What do I do now to improve myself in this area?

_____
_____

On a scale of 1 to 5, with 5 meaning "I am using all my personal energy on this dimension" and 1 meaning "I am doing nothing at all," how would you rate your focus on this dimension?   **1   2   3   4   5**

Dimension 2: The Soul

Definition:

_____
_____

What do I do now to improve myself in this area?

_____
_____

On a scale of 1 to 5, with 5 meaning "I am using all my personal energy on this dimension" and 1 meaning "I am doing nothing at all," how would you rate your focus on this dimension?   **1   2   3   4   5**

Dimension 3: The Spirit

Definition:

_____

_____

What do I do now to improve myself in this area?

_____

_____

On a scale of 1 to 5, with 5 meaning "I am using all my personal energy on this dimension" and 1 meaning I am doing nothing at all," how would you rate your focus on this dimension?   **1   2   3   4   5**

MISTAKES TO AVOID

As you use this workbook, you will find activities that help you focus on developing those skills. You will also have opportunities to reflect on behaviors that may keep you from achieving the level of success for which you strive.

Which one of these **Mistakes to Avoid** is the one you need to work on changing in your life?

Skill: Fear and Anxiety

- ❖ **Assuming you are incapable of finding the courage to face your fears or stretching beyond your self-imposed limitations.** Result: Miss the chance. Condemn yourself to a life sentence of fear-bound captivity without benefit of experiencing life fully.
- ❖ **Ignoring all evidence that your fears are exaggerated, generalized, or unfounded.** Result: Remain imprisoned by irrational fear; allow it to impede or stop you from enjoying life, pursuing goals, or realizing dreams. Miss the chance to explore the validity and scope of your fear, work through it, repair the damage, and reclaim those things you may have lost or abandoned while in its unrelenting grip.

Skill: Stress

- ❖ **Making commitments first and asking questions later.** Result: Learn too late that you have taken on more than you can handle. Struggle to meet the unrealistic deadlines and expectations others set for you.
- ❖ **Responding with "yes" when you really wanted to say "no."** Result: Put your name at the top of the to-call list for those who are willing to delegate. Please others at the expense of your family or those with whom you have made previous commitments. Confuse the word "no" with selfishness.

Skill: Time Management

- ❖ **Attempting to work without forethought or planning.** Result: Spend inordinate amounts of time trying to remember what it is you are supposed to accomplish. Then, work hard only to realize you have neglected the most important tasks, to the dismay and disappointment of others and, possibly, the demise of your own unrecorded priorities.
- ❖ **Avoiding opportunities to think and reflect. Working or playing until you drop.** Result: Live reactively rather than proactively. Be unprepared to make important decisions. Delay or let others make important life decisions for you. Wonder why your relationships with others seem superficial and unrewarding.

BRINGING BALANCE TO A CHAOTIC LIFE

In the following article, Chris Widener (co-author of **Twelve Pillars**) offers advice on how to balance the three dimensions of personal health. Read the short narrative and then answer the reflective questions that follow.

If I had to make a composite question that gets at the heart of the question that I am asked most frequently, it would be this:

How can I manage my time more effectively and bring balance to my life in regard to work, family, friends, and social obligations?

With this in mind, I want to give us some thoughts to focus us in on the answer to that question.

I am convinced that the most important thing we must do is to be acutely aware of the reasons I should manage my time and bring balance to my life. In fact, most of us really know "how" to do it, don't we? Then why don't we? I think it comes to the issue of having a powerful motivating factor or reason. Below are two of mine that keep me motivated:

A life of accomplishment. *When I am old and unable to get out with the young folks anymore, I want to be able to look back on my life and say that I accomplished much and that my life benefited others. That is why I do what I do now. It is what drives me to pursue what I pursue with a passion and vigor. It is why I bring my life into balance in many areas so I can achieve much in many areas.*

A legacy. *Here is a powerful motivating image that I picture with regularity: Picture a family gathering five years after your death. What will it look like? What will the people be talking about? How will they remember you? What will be the quality of their lives and how will you have been instrumental in that? These are questions that we can for the most part, answer now by how we live our lives (for better or for worse). Our lives make a difference in the lives of others! This is a tremendous reason to bring my life into balance!*

Once we answer the "Why" question, and root it firmly in our minds and hearts, we come to the "hows."

First, we sit down and prioritize. Have you ever taken a couple of hours and listed everything that you are involved in or could be involved in and then prioritized it by importance? You may come up with a hundred items but that is okay. You will want to separate them into some categories as well, such as Work, Family, Health, Friends, Hobbies, Spiritual, Financial, Intellectual, Emotional, etc.

Now you have something to look at and see what is important. This will help you in the process of eliminating areas from your life that you are spending time on that you shouldn't be. And that is an important part: Frustration comes when we get involved in something that isn't a priority and we kick ourselves the whole time we do it. If we stick to priorities, we eliminate much of that.

The next step is to learn the most powerful word in the human language: No. Just look in the mirror and practice saying that word with a smile on your face.

This may be the most important part – learning to decline opportunity. It all depends on whether or not it fits in with our priorities.

Here is the principle that drives this: Good is the enemy of the best.

There are lots of good things we can spend our time on. But because they replace those things that would be the best things we could spend our time on, they become our enemy. They become counter-productive to a successful and balanced life.

So ask yourself: Is this good? Or is it the best? Do the best you can to stick to the best!

Schedule your time. The more we fly by the seat of our pants, the more apt we are to lose control of our time. If we schedule out our time, we can become a bit more objective and bring our lives into balance. For example, you may make it your goal to be home by six o'clock every night. In your schedule book, you write in that you have an appointment at six. You schedule to leave the office at five-thirty. Now when a co-worker comes in with an "opportunity" for you to work on, you say, "Sorry, I have an appointment at six that I can't break. Let's get together on it first thing in the morning." Scheduling your time, coupled with saying "no," will do wonders for bringing your life into balance!

Another aspect for us to look at is the area of external pressure that causes us to be out of balance. For example, financial obligations may be what keep us working too much. So we should look at those obligations and see if we can eliminate or reduce them.

The last thing I would challenge you with is to give some thought as to what the secret pleasures of being out of balance may be. For example, sometimes we let ourselves over commit because we don't like conflict. Peace is our secret pleasure.

Sometimes we allow ourselves to become out of balance because we like it when people say, "Boy, she sure is a dynamo. Look how busy she is." Admiration from others is our secret pleasure.

In review:

Find the right reasons

Set priorities

Learn to say "no"

Understand that the good is the enemy of the best

Schedule your time

Manage External pressures

Be aware of internal "secret pleasures"

(by Chris Widener)

1. Chris describes his reasons for bringing balance to his life. What is your reason? (Perhaps it is the reason you bought this workbook!)
   _____
   _____

2. What do you think about the statement "Good is the enemy of the best"?
   _____
   _____

3. What tools do you use now to schedule your time?
   _____
   _____

4. Name one thing you could do to improve the way you manage your time:
   _____
   _____

5. External pressures can keep you from having a balanced life. Describe your greatest external pressure:
   _____
   _____

   Name one thing you can do to manage that pressure:
   _____
   _____

6. Secret pleasures can keep you from having a balanced life. Describe your greatest secret pleasure:
   _____
   _____

   Name one thing you can do to manage that pleasure:
   _____
   _____

SETTING PRIORITIES

In his article, "Bringing Balance to a Chaotic Life," Chris Widener suggests taking time to list everything you are currently involved in or could be involved in within your life, and then prioritizing them by importance.

On the following blank page, begin by brainstorming your own list. Think of such aspects as:

- Work
- Family
- Friends
- Hobbies
- Household/Community
- Spiritual
- Financial
- Education/Intellectual

You may want to put each item on a post-it note and arrange them on a table or white board to categorize. Sort them by importance to you.

Once you have prioritized these items, look at them again and indicate how much time you spend on each one using the following rating scale:

1 – I spend a lot of time on this activity (20 hours or more each week)
2 – I spend a moderate amount of time on this activity (10-15 hours each week)
3 – I spend a small amount of time on this activity (5-10 hours each week)
4 – I spend almost no time on this activity (less than 5 hours each week)

Ask yourself these questions:

- Are there areas or activities on which you spend a lot of time that are not very high on your list of priorities?

  _____

- Are there some activities you rated as a 3 or 4 that are at the top of your priority list?

  _____

- What can you do to change and bring your life in balance?

  _____

MY PRIORITIES

MY LIST OF GOALS

In **Twelve Pillars**, Charlie reminds Michael that we function best when we live in balance. Are you in balance? **Set three short-term goals for the next week to bring balance to all three dimensions of your personal health.**

BODY

1. _____
2. _____
3. _____

SOUL

1. _____
2. _____
3. _____

SPIRIT

1. _____
2. _____
3. _____

Listed below are the Critical Skills needed to be proficient in this Pillar. Also listed are the Additional Essential Skills needed for mastery.

Critical Skills	Additional Essential Skills
Fear and Anxiety	Optimism/Positive Attitude and Ambition
Stress	Courage
Time Management	Accountability
Prioritizing	Responsibility

Pillar Three

"Time, effort, and imagination must be summoned constantly to keep any relationship flourishing and growing."

Before you begin this portion of the **Twelve Pillars Workbook**, read or reread Chapter 3, *The Gift of Relationships,* of **Twelve Pillars**.

Pillar Three

The third Pillar of Success is to make the most of the Gift of Relationships... relationships represent the most beautiful highs of life as well as some of the most tormented lows of life. It is all what you make of them." (Charlie, ***Twelve Pillars****)*

In this chapter, you will be considering many aspects of building and maintaining relationships, learning how strong relationships must be rooted in mutual commitment.

We use the term "commitment" to mean many things, ranging from keeping an appointment to keeping faith in our relationships with others. The word connotes different things in different situations. In some, it means obligation, duty, responsibility, or liability. In others, it means steadfastness, loyalty, and dedication. Although different, these nuances all infer principles that point to strength of character. When we consistently keep our personal and professional commitments, we earn the trust and respect of others. They know that we will follow through and do our very best to deliver what we promise when we promise it.

Admittedly, legitimate unforeseeable events can occur that disrupt even our best-laid plans and thwart our ability to meet a commitment. When this happens, the most effective remedy is a proactive response:

- Notify all concerned parties immediately.

- Identify the potential impact on timetables and deliverables.

- Propose alternative options, including realistic timelines and deliverables.

- Follow through.

True emergencies are a rare and understandable part of life. Chronic emergencies and repeated patterns of unfulfilled promises indicate poor planning and flawed time management or a lack of self-discipline and credibility.

In a world filled with irresponsibility, broken promises, and excuses, the individual who staunchly stands by his or her commitments to others is a rare treasure.

CRITICAL OUTCOMES FOR PILLAR THREE:
- Identifying strategies for growing and nurturing relationships
- Evaluating progress of short-term goals and reevaluating direction.

IMPROVING YOUR RELATIONSHIPS: TIME, EFFORT AND IMAGINATION

In **Twelve Pillars**, Charlie compares relationships to gardening. In both situations, three elements are essential: time, effort, and imagination. Both also require hard work and consistent maintenance to keep them healthy.

How is your relationship "garden" growing? Read the following questions and write your responses in the space provided.

Skill: Time (Time Management)

Consider your priority list from the last chapter. Choose one of your top priorities from the last chapter and write it in the space below.

_____

_____

How can you improve the quantity and quality of time you spend on the relationship that supports that priority?

_____

_____

Create a short-term goal that you can achieve within the next week to make those improvements:

_____

_____

Skill: Effort (Prioritizing and Support)

Describe the highest-priority relationship in your life right now.

_____

_____

What kind of effort is needed to improve the support you provide to the other person in that relationship?

_____

_____

Create a short-term goal that you can achieve within the next week to increase the effort you put into that relationship:

_____

_____

Skill: Imagination (Creative Thinking)

Consider your priority list from the last chapter again. Choose another one of your top priorities from the last chapter and write it in the space below.

_____

_____

Describe the relationship that currently exists which supports that priority:

_____

_____

Now imagine how that relationship COULD be. Describe one thing that you could do to make that relationship the way you imagine it:

_____

_____

MISTAKES TO AVOID

As you use this workbook, you will find activities that help you focus on developing those skills. You will also have opportunities to reflect on behaviors that may keep you from achieving the level of success for which you strive.

*Which one of these **Mistakes to Avoid** is the one you need to work on changing in your life?*

Skill: Commitment

- ❖ **Refusing to commit or treating commitments and promises as changeable, whimsical propositions.** Result: Encourage others to see you as the "artful dodger" – immature and unwilling to make commitments.

Skill: Time Management

- ❖ **Misinterpreting "quality time" for activity-laden time.** Result: Stay busier than a bumblebee. Unlike the bee, miss the beauty and fragrance of life's flowers.

Skill: Prioritizing

- ❖ **Blaming others for your inability to establish or commit to priorities.** Result: Watch helplessly as the people and things you treasure gradually abandon you as you continue wandering pointlessly through life. Blame those who desert you along the way for your losses.

Skill: Support Others

- ❖ **Taking action without asking how you can best provide support.** Result: Miss the rewards that come from giving for the benefit of others.

Skill: Diversity

- ❖ **Attempting to force your beliefs and values upon others.** Result: Change nothing. Foster distrust and resentment. Observe how people will avoid your company.

Skill: Respect

- ❖ **Withholding respect from others due to their differences in background, appearance, beliefs, or abilities.** Result: Invite a lack of respect from others. Display your ignorance and close-minded values.

ANCHOR YOUR RELATIONSHIPS

In the following article, Chris Widener (co-author of **Twelve Pillars**) reflects on the basic principles needed to develop and maintain strong relationships. Read the short narrative and then answer the reflective questions that follow.

I heard a speaker recently who was talking about how to maintain strong relationships. As I listened to his basic principle, I realized that it is true in all of our life situations, be it work, family etc. And let's face it, relationships are what make the world go 'round. So strong healthy relationships will make your work more enjoyable, and prosperous, and will make your family and friend relationships better as well.

What was the principle? The speaker said that each point of connection is like an anchor in the relationship, and the more connections you have, the stronger the relationship will be. He calls one-connection relationships "Simplex," and multi-connection relationships, "Multiplex." The strongest relationships are multiplex.

There is also the idea that some connections are stronger than others and so you want as many connections as possible and you want those connections to be as strong as they can be as well. Confused? Let's put some legs on this. We'll take a business situation and we'll take a family situation to illustrate the principle.

Anchoring work relationships.

Let's say you sell insurance. A guy walks in and says, "I would like to purchase some term life insurance." You have a simplex relationship. The connection is that you both want him to have insurance. As you get to know him better and get information from him, you realize that you have a multiplex relationship growing and the chance that your business relationship will grow is improving.

"You grew up in Iowa? Me too!"

"You like to golf? Me too!"

"Your wife and you like to go to the opera? So do we! We should go together sometime."

The multiple connections are anchoring your relationship.

Anchoring a family relationship.

Let's take a marriage in trouble. Chances are that at one time, the relationship was multiplex. Because of time, work, and other stresses, the marriage has deteriorated to the point where both are thinking, "What did I marry this person for?" Or "Why do I stay?" The chances are that now the relationship is simplex. Maybe it is that the one connection is that they want to do right by the kids and so they "Tough it out." What is the answer? I believe that it is regaining a multiplex relationship. Work hard to make those other anchoring connections. Did you used to play tennis together before the kids came along? Go play tennis together on a regular basis. Do you both have a common interest in a specific cause or charity, but time hasn't allowed you to pursue it? Take the time! It will anchor your relationship again!

I think you get the point.

Take some time to think about your current relationships. Are they as multiplex as they can be or as they used to be? Think about the new relationships you will make in the coming weeks or months. Think of ways you can make them strong by finding multiple connections, securing deeper and more fulfilling relationships.

Make your relationships "multiplex" and you make them strong, with an anchor that will not let them go!

(by Chris Widener)

1. What is the "basic principle" Chris describes in this article?

   _____

   _____

2. What is a simplex relationship? Give an example of a simplex relationship in your life.

   _____

   _____

3. What is a multiplex relationship?

   _____

   _____

4. How can you change the simplex relationship from the question above into a multiplex one?

   _____

   _____

ANALYZING AND PROBLEM SOLVING YOUR RELATIONSHIPS

In **Twelve Pillars**, you read about the importance of relationships in building a successful life. Reflecting on the time, effort, and imagination needed to improve them is an important first step. Analyzing a relationship's strengths, weaknesses, opportunities, and challenges (threats) is another way to determine how to work with others to achieve your goals. This process is called a "SWOT Analysis" (named for the first letters of each of the four quadrants of the chart) and can be used in any situation where problem solving and analysis is needed.

Complete a SWOT for a relationship in your personal and professional environment. Fill in the blanks below:

STRENGTHS (What works well in this relationship?) **Example**: I **respect** this person.	WEAKNESSES (What doesn't work well in this relationship?) **Example**: I don't know how to **support** this person effectively.
OPPORTUNITIES (What potential exists for improving this relationship?) **Example**: We are both **committed** to making this relationship work.	THREATS (What might keep us from achieving that potential?) **Example**: We are so **diverse** in our beliefs about some things.

Once you have completed the chart, reflect on how the Strengths might help you achieve the Opportunities and overcome the Threats. What can you do to strengthen the Weaknesses?

MY LIST OF GOALS – CHECKING IN

In the last two workbook chapters, you ended your activities by writing up some short-term goals to work on. In the space below, write each of those goals, the amount of time that has elapsed since you set them, and the progress you made towards achieving them. Indicate whether this is a goal that you want to continue to work on, and if so, what your next step will be now.

My Goals	How much time has passed	Progress made towards achieving my goal	My next step for this goal

Listed below are the Critical Skills needed to be proficient in this Pillar. Also listed are the Additional Essential Skills needed for mastery.

Critical Skills	Additional Essential Skills
Commitment	Adversity
Support Others	Team
Creative Thinking	Leadership
Diversity	Speaking
Respect	Listening
Problem Solving	Optimism/Positive Attitude and Ambition

Pillar Four

*"The major reason for setting a goal is
for what it makes of you to accomplish it."*

Before you begin this portion of the **Twelve Pillars Workbook**, read or reread Chapter 4, *Achieve Your Goals*, of **Twelve Pillars**.

Pillar Four

"Start by changing your direction. You are where you are, but you don't have to stay there. Choose where you want to go and then build out your plan for getting there." (Charlie, **Twelve Pillars**)

Deciding what you want to do and then getting started – this is one of the most powerful lessons in life, according to Charlie in **Twelve Pillars**. This advice about goal setting and following through is critical to success on the job and in daily life. Whether it is planning a major office presentation, preparing a meal, troubleshooting a corporate-wide software glitch, organizing a group to undertake a new initiative, or completing a customer's production order, most of us have projects that need planning. Goal setting is just a variation on project planning. In each case, we must: 1) identify our goals and desired outcomes; 2) plan our time; 3) acquire and organize our resources; 4) prioritize and complete tasks in a logical sequence; and 5) evaluate the results of our efforts.

Some projects are relatively simple and require minimal planning and resources to achieve the desired outcomes. Others are more complex, requiring significant planning, resources, task coordination, monitoring, and assessment. Regardless of the relative simplicity or complexity of a project, our ability to establish goals, plan strategies, manage resources, perform and delegate tasks, and evaluate processes and outcomes will determine the relative success or failure of our projects.

This is also true of goal setting for your life. By setting long-range goals, you are stating your expected outcomes for your life. Planning your time means identifying and prioritizing short-range and mini-goals in the form of tasks that will help you achieve the long-range goal. All of us have resources to draw from in achieving our goals, and we must have ways to periodically measure how far we have come in achieving those plans.

CRITICAL OUTCOMES FOR PILLAR FOUR:

- Identifying long-range goals and breaking them into smaller tasks and timelines.
- Identifying elements of Project Planning

GOAL #1: IDENTIFY YOUR 100 GOALS

In **Twelve Pillars**, Charlie tells Michael that the first step to setting a goal is to "write it down." He explains that this action does two things: first, because you have to write it down, you have to actually have a goal. Second, by writing it down, it brings the goal into reality. Charlie challenges Michael to write down the 100 things he wants to accomplish before he dies. In the space below, begin your list of your 100 Life Goals. Keep this list in a place where you can be reminded of it often.

Before I die, I want to:

MISTAKES TO AVOID

As you use this workbook, you will find activities that help you focus on developing those skills. You will also have opportunities to reflect on behaviors that may keep you from achieving the level of success for which you strive.

Which one of these **Mistakes to Avoid** is the one you need to work on changing in your life?

Skill: Project Planning/Goal Setting

- ❖ **Moving forward without a clear understanding of the goal.** Result: Expend a great deal of energy to achieve the wrong outcomes. Waste precious time and resources. Delay progress toward desired goals to the overall dismay of all stakeholders.
- ❖ **Neglecting to consider overall project goals and timelines when planning, performing, or delegating tasks.** Result: Experience the constant state of frustration and confusion that accompanies this helter-skelter approach to task completion. Expend valuable time and energy retracking tasks, hoping you will somehow manage to tame an out-of-control process into one that will meet the established goals and timelines.

Skill: Decision Making

- ❖ **Allowing others to make decisions for you, and then complaining about the decision.** Result: Give up personal responsibility, but criticize and frustrate the decision maker.
- ❖ **Making decisions based only on emotions rather than including reliable data and information.** Result: Impede progress, generate uncertainty, undermine confidence, and please no one.

Skill: Prioritizing

- ❖ **Performing the easiest or most pleasant tasks first, regardless of their importance.** Result: Experience mounting stress and anxiety as the deadlines for priority tasks approach. Find yourself lost for words or offering lame excuses when asked to justify poor quality work or unmet timelines.
- ❖ **Neglecting considering your priorities when making decisions or taking on additional responsibilities.** Result: Load yourself with more responsibilities than you can possibly fulfill in the given timeframe. Grovel, beg, or growl to convince others that your poor planning has become their emergency.

ALL YOU WANT IS WITHIN YOUR REACH

Whether you are setting life goals or planning a project, the key to succeeding is making the choice to do so. In the following article, Chris Widener (co-author of **Twelve Pillars**) challenges each of us to make the decisions that will lead to success. Read the short narrative and then answer the reflective questions that follow.

> *If there is one thing that I believe with all my heart it is that you can have any life you choose to. You can live the life you have always dreamed of.*
>
> *We live in a period of unparalleled opportunity in human history. Think about it: Just one hundred years ago, most people really only had five or six options when it came to deciding what they would do with their lives. For most, they didn't even have the knowledge that they could do anything other than take over their father's farm when they turned eighteen!*
>
> *But today a person living in the western world (and many other areas of the world as well) can choose to do virtually anything they want to! The key is the word "choose."*
>
> *You see, the world is within your reach. Any job you want can be yours if you decide. All of the opportunities are there for the taking. The question is whether or not you will take.*
>
> *You say, "But Chris, you just don't understand. I'm thirty-eight years old with two kids and I have bills to pay. I make $28,000 a year. I can't just go become a doctor and make big money!"*
>
> *And I say, "Yes you can! If you decide to. If you will take action you can become a doctor or anything else you want to. We live in a day and age when virtually anything is possible."*
>
> *For the sake of highlighting this principle, let's look at the above example. How would this person change careers? Simple. Here is the process in specific action steps:*
>
> 1. *Find out from a medical school what classes you would need to take to get in. Chances are your college major would need some rounding out or if you didn't go to college, you would need to do so. Maximum time to do this: 3 days.*
> 2. *Now, go to school. Maximum time to do this: 4 years.*
> 3. *Now, medical school and residency. Maximum time to do this: 6 years.*
> 4. *Begin practicing medicine.*
>
> *At this point you would be forty-eight years old. That leaves you seventeen years to practice. Now let's see the impact it has on your life:*
>
> 1. *You get to pursue your dream, making you and your family MUCH happier.*
> 2. *You will make, on average, $100,000 more per year. The difference here is manifold! If you stayed where you were, you would have earned $28,000 a year for twenty-seven years and would earn $756,000. If you left and*

pursued your dream you would earn $128,000 for seventeen years (That's if you took ten years to make the transition. Most would be less.) and your earnings would be $2,176,000! This is a difference of $1,420,000! And this doesn't even take into consideration the amounts you would earn on investments on the difference in incomes.

So is it possible? Yes. Does it take time? Yes. Is it hard? Yes. Is it scary? Yes, and that is why most people won't do it.

It isn't for lack of opportunity. It is usually because of one of the following:

Lack of vision.

Lack of tenacity.

Fear.

The truth is that you can do anything you want to. Stop telling yourself excuses! Go to battle against a lack of vision! Pick yourself up and get tenacious! Look fear in the face and stand up to it! Your whole life depends on it, my friend!

The choice is yours. Will you continue to limp along in life because you don't have the courage to run for your dream? Will you continue to allow the fear of poverty keep you from pursuing the riches, both materially and emotionally, that lay within the vision you have of what your life could be?

You CAN live the life you have always dreamed of. All you want is within your reach. But to pick it up, you must first empty your hands of what they already hold. Then you must reach for it, take a hold of it, and possess it!

(by Chris Widener)

1. What is your greatest life-long dream?

   _____

   _____

2. Is it on your list of priorities from earlier chapters?

   _____

   _____

3. Is it on your list of 100 Things to Do Before I Die? _____ If it is not on both of these lists, why not?

   _____

   _____

4. In this article, Chris concludes by saying that to live the life you always dreamed of, "you must first empty your hands of what they already hold." What are you willing to let go of to achieve the success you seek?

_____

_____

How does that make you feel about striving for that goal?

_____

_____

DEFINING MY LIST OF GOALS

In **Twelve Pillars**, Charlie explains how Michael can break down a long-range goal into smaller, more manageable mid-range, short-range, and even micro-goals. Choose one of your goals from a previous chapter. If it is a short-range goal (1 year or less), expand it to be part of a longer-range goal. If it is a long-range goal, break it down into smaller ones. Be sure to put the date by which you expect it to be completed.

My Long-Range Goal (5 to 10 years from now):

_____ By _____

One Mid-Range Goal needed to ultimately achieve the Long-Range Goal (in the next 2-5 years):

_____ By _____

One Short-Range Goal needed to ultimately achieve the Long-Range Goal (in the next 1-2 years):

_____ By _____

Micro-Goals:

- **What can I do in the next six months to ultimately achieve my Long-Range Goal?**

    _____ By _____

- **What can I do in the next two weeks to ultimately achieve my Long-Range Goal?**

    _____ By _____

- **What can I do in the next 24 hours to ultimately achieve my Long-Range Goal?**

    _____ By _____

Listed below are the Critical Skills needed to be proficient in this Pillar. Also listed are the Additional Essential Skills needed for mastery.

Critical Skills	Additional Essential Skills
Project Planning/Goal Setting	Organization
Prioritizing	Support Others
Decision Making	Procrastination
Responsibility	Writing

Pillar Five

"Every day has many opportunities
but only one best opportunity."

Before you begin this portion of the **Twelve Pillars Workbook**, read or reread Chapter 5, *The Proper Use of Time*, of **Twelve Pillars**.

Pillar Five

*"...Something will master and something will serve. Either you run your day or the day runs you. Either you control your time or it controls you. Take your pick." (Charlie, **Twelve Pillars**)*

Time and its mysteries have intrigued humanity since the beginning of civilization. While it is not a visible entity, time is observable and measurable through the changes that occur around and within us. Like Charlie in **Twelve Pillars**, some people value time as a precious gift or commodity. Others, like Michael, experience it as a burdensome and relentless taskmaster. In most cases, an individual's perception of time is a direct result of his or her ability to manage it.

To make the best use of our time at work, just as in our lives, we must first identify our goals and prioritize our tasks according to their importance and established timelines. When given the option to establish timelines, we should carefully consider the full scope of the project or task in light of our other obligations before committing to a deadline. We must then establish a working balance between the required number of tasks, available resources, and our ability to perform the tasks to acceptable standards. When appropriate, we should delegate tasks to others. Delegation of tasks might require an initial investment of additional time for training, but the investment will prove worthwhile in the long term.

Our personal values, goals, and priorities should guide the manner in which we use our time away from work. Ultimately, the value and benefit of time spent, not the number of activities we squeeze into it, will determine its quality. Wasting time will cause a lifetime of regrets. Use it well to experience life's fullest rewards.

CRITICAL OUTCOMES FOR PILLAR FIVE:
- Identifying time management strategies
- Applying those strategies to personal and work life
- Setting timelines and meeting deadlines

TRACKING YOUR TIME TO TAKE CONTROL

Activity logs help you to analyze how you actually spend your time. The first time you use an activity log you may be shocked to see the amount of time that you waste! Memory is a very poor guide when it comes to this, as it can be too easy to forget time spent reading junk mail, talking to colleagues, making coffee, eating lunch, etc.

You may also be unaware that your energy levels may vary through the day. In fact, most people function at different levels of effectiveness at different times. Your effectiveness may vary depending on the amount of sugar in your blood, the length of time since you last took a break, routine distractions, stress, discomfort, or a range of other factors. There is also some good evidence that you have daily rhythms of alertness and energy. **Use the charts on the following pages to track your time, or make your own.**

Keeping an Activity Log for several days helps you to understand how you spend your time and when you perform at your best. Without interfering with your behavior any further than you have to, note down the things you do as you do them. Every time you change activities, whether opening mail, working, making coffee, gossiping with colleagues or whatever, note down the time of the change.

Once you have logged your time for a few days, analyze the log. You may be alarmed to see the length of time you spend performing low-priority tasks! You may also see that you are energetic in some parts of the day and flat in other parts. A lot of this can depend on the rest breaks you take, the times and amounts you eat, and quality of your nutrition.

TIME USE CHART

Week of: _____

Use this chart over a one-week period. Record everything you do in half-hour increments. At the end of the week, complete the Time Summary Chart to see what you spent your time doing all week.

Time	Mon	Tues	Wed	Thurs	Fri	Sat	Sun
6:00 am							
6:30							
7:00							
7:30							
8:00							
8:30							
9:00							
9:30							
10:00							
10:30							
11:00							
11:30							
NOON							
12:30 pm							
1:00							
1:30							

Time	Mon	Tues	Wed	Thurs	Fri	Sat	Sun
2:00							
2:30							
3:00							
3:30							
4:00							
4:30							
5:00							
5:30							
6:00							
6:30							
7:00							
7:30							
8:00							
8:30							
9:00							
9:30							
10:00							
10:30							
11:00							
11:30							
Midnight							

TIME USE SUMMARY CHART

Summarize your activities from your week's worth of time charts. Put the hours in each column and the total at the bottom. Some categories are suggested on the left-hand column, with subcategories as an example. Write in whatever ones are appropriate for you.

SUMMARY OF ACTIVITIES									
ACTIVITY		MON	TUE	WED	THU	FRI	SAT	SUN	TOTAL
Home/Family	House								
	Spouse/Partner								
	Children/Relatives								
	Spiritual								
	Pets								
Work									
Personal	Friends								
	Social & Recreational								
	Community								
	Education/Intellectual								
	Hobbies								
Health-Related	Eating, Bathing, etc.								
	Exercise								
	Sleep								
Other									
Total Hours									

Reflect on how this compares with the Priority list you created in Pillar Two. Are your highest-rated priorities the ones where you are spending the most time? Do you need to make adjustments to reach your Long-Range Goals?

MISTAKES TO AVOID

As you use this workbook, you will find activities that help you focus on developing those skills. You will also have opportunities to reflect on behaviors that may keep you from achieving the level of success for which you strive.

Which one of these **Mistakes to Avoid** is the one you need to work on changing in your life?

Skill: Time Management

- **Saying "Yes" when you should say "No."** Result: Place yourself at the top of others' volunteer list. Experience the demoralizing duo of remorse and resentment when you realize you have once again accepted more responsibilities that you can realistically fulfill.
- **Abandoning or ignoring priorities; attacking work randomly.** Result: Prepare to face the wrath of unhappy co-workers, supervisors, and clients without any viable means of escape or self-defense.
- **Owning the latest time management tools and gadgets, then leaving them untouched.** Result: Miss important meetings, commitments, and deadlines. Convince others that you are at the least forgetful, or at the most incompetent.

Skill: Accountability

- **Making commitments without due consideration.** Result: Promise too much, too soon, to too many people. Panic, take ineffective shortcuts, and fail to deliver what you promised.
- **Acting now, planning later.** Result: Get nowhere fast.

Skill: Responsibility

- **Allowing pride to keep you from seeking assistance when you realize you cannot meet your responsibilities.** Result: Needing help is not a weakness unless you ask for it, receive it, and don't learn from it. Every accomplished man or woman has achieved success with help from others; failure is a certainty if you insist on going it alone.
- **Allowing fear of failure to keep you from accepting responsibility.** Result: Risk nothing and gain nothing. Deny yourself a better, more meaningful life.

THINKING LIKE A FARMER

Sometimes when we focus on time management, we can get caught up in tracking the day-to-day, hour-to-hour, even minute-to-minute activities of our lives. In the following article, Jim Rohn (co-author of **Twelve Pillars**) takes a step back to consider time as seasons of life. Read the short narrative and then answer the reflective questions that follow.

> *One of the difficulties we face in our industrialized age is the fact we've lost our sense of seasons. Unlike the farmer whose priorities change with the seasons, we have become impervious to the natural rhythm of life. As a result, we have our priorities out of balance. Let me illustrate what I mean:*
>
> *For a farmer, springtime is his most active time. It's then when he must work around the clock, up before the sun and still toiling at the stroke of midnight. He must keep his equipment running at full capacity because he has but a small window of time for the planting of his crop. Eventually winter comes when there is less for him to do to keep him busy.*
>
> *There is a lesson here. Learn to use the seasons of life. Decide when to pour it on and when to ease back, when to take advantage and when to let things ride. It's easy to keep going from nine to five year in and year out and lose a natural sense of priorities and cycles. Don't let one year blend into another in a seemingly endless parade of tasks and responsibilities. Keep your eye on your own seasons, lest you lose sight of value and substance.*
>
> *(by Jim Rohn)*

1. Reflect on how you currently manage your time. Do you change your energy and level of time commitment based on your goals, or are you getting lost in the "endless parade of tasks and responsibilities"?

   _____
   _____

2. Are there any areas of your life now where you follow the "seasons of life" in how you manage your time (sports, gardening, other hobbies, animals, family)?

   _____
   _____

3. If you were to change your schedule to the "seasons of life" that best support your long-range goals, what is the first thing you would need to do?

   _____
   _____

4. Look back at your responses in Pillar Two (*page 18 of that section*). What tools did you list as being used now to schedule your time?

   _____
   _____

5. Now that you have read and reflected further on how you manage your time, what changes (if any) will you commit to making in how you schedule and manage your activities?

   _____
   _____

PLAN, DO, CHECK, ACT (PDCA)

Walter Andrew Shewhart (1891 - 1967) first originated the PDCA problem solving process. Dr. William Edwards Deming (1900 - 1993), a student of Walter Shewhart's, popularized the process in Japan where it is known as the Deming Cycle.

There are four stages in the problem solving process: Plan, Do, Check, Act

Plan	• Obtain accurate and complete data and input to determine whether a problem exists.
	• Identify and examine the people-, process-, and systems-related causes of the problem and how they are impacted.
	• Determine whether the probable causes of the problem are events or patterns and whether the problem can be solved or only managed.
	• Develop an action plan that includes the goal you want to achieve, success indicators, cost/benefit analysis, risk and disruption assessment, and resources.
Do	• Implement the solution, step by step, and monitor each step for functionality, efficiencies, and/or effectiveness.
Check	• Follow up with the people, processes, and/or systems involved to evaluate your success.
	• Get experienced input as to the functionality, efficiencies, and/or effectiveness, and make the necessary adjustments to attain your goal.
Act	• Adopt the solution if you achieved the desired results.
	• If you didn't achieve the desired results, go back and check the progress of each step and find what went wrong.
	• Make the necessary adjustments and implement the corrected steps.
	• Continue to monitor the solution, and make adjustments as needed.

The PDCA process is useful in both work and personal settings. For this activity, consider one of your Short-Term Goals that you want to accomplish in the next two weeks. What problems might be associated with achieving that Short-Term Goal? Refer to the Plan-Do-Check-Act chart on the previous page as you answer the questions and work through the activity.

Short-Term Goal:

_____
_____

Brief Summary of the Problem in Achieving that Goal in the next two weeks:

_____
_____

Plan:

Is the problem primarily related to a person? _____ A process? _____ A system? _____ A combination of one or more of these? _____

Managing a problem means that you might not be able to change the person, process, or system, but you can adjust your plan so that you can find a solution. For example, you might be able to find an exception to a rule, call in a favor from someone in authority, or go through legal or organizational means to resolve it.

Can you solve this problem or must it be "managed"? _____

Action plans can be simple or very complex. For this activity, describe in just a few sentences what your plan for resolving this problem will be:

_____
_____
_____
_____

Do:

Try out your action plan in the next few days. When you have taken your first steps, write in the space below how well it worked and what you might do differently next time.

_____
_____
_____
_____

Check:

The third step of this process is to look at the results of your first try and make whatever adjustments are needed to be successful. If your plan worked the first time, congratulations! However, most of the time there are parts of a plan that didn't run as smoothly as you might have imagined or unforeseen circumstances forced you to change your plan in mid-implementation. You might want to ask others for feedback on the parts of your plan that did not go as well as you would have liked. In the space below, reflect on your plan's success and what you or others would advise that you try to do differently.

_____
_____
_____
_____

Act:

This is the step where you have worked out all the problems and are completely successful. You may reach this stage on the first try or it may take several attempts. If the process to reach this Short-Term Goal is one that you want to adopt for other problems, this is where you can continue to monitor and make adjustments the next time you use it.

MY LIST OF BEST OPPORTUNITIES

In **Twelve Pillars**, Charlie advises Michael that days are expensive. "When you spend a day, you have one less day to spend. So make sure you spend each one wisely." He goes on to explain that every day has many opportunities, but only one "best opportunity"; that is, the opportunity that aligns with your overall goals should be what you spend your time on.

In this activity, list your Long-Range Goal (5 to 10 years out) in the space below. Then go back through your Time Use Chart completed earlier in this chapter and list all the "best opportunities"; you had this week that align with reaching that goal:

My Long-Range Goal:

_____

_____

Best Opportunities I took advantage of this week:

_____

_____

_____

How many Best Opportunities did you list? _____

What can you do next week to improve that number?

_____

_____

_____

Listed below are the Critical Skills needed to be proficient in this Pillar. Also listed are the Additional Essential Skills needed for mastery.

Critical Skills	Additional Essential Skills
Problem Solving	Observation
Accountability	Leadership
Time Management	Project Planning/Goal Setting
Responsibility	Organization

Pillar Six

"Don't join an easy crowd; you won't grow.

Go where the expectations and the demands to perform are high."

Before you begin this portion of the **Twelve Pillars Workbook**, read or reread Chapter 6, *Surround Yourself With the Best People*, of **Twelve Pillars**.

Pillar Six

*"Every relationship you have is an association, and each association has either a positive, neutral, or negative effect on you. So a person who wants to achieve success has to constantly make a determination about what kind of relationship it is and how to approach that relationship." (Charlie, **Twelve Pillars**)*

Many of us heard as children that "we become like those we associate with." Our parents didn't want us hanging out with the troublemakers or unmotivated kids; they knew that if we did, we'd turn out just like them. It's no different as an adult. A common refrain heard among successful people is that "like minds attract." In other words, observe who people associate with, and you'll get a good read on their values and morals, as well as their ambition and attitude.

Charlie points out to Michael how important it is for him to choose his friends and close business associates wisely. In his wisdom, Charlie knows that a college education is not the key to success. The key is the influence you have with people who are where you want to go and are who you want to be.

If living a rewarding and productive life is 90 percent attitude, as Charlie explains to Michael, then academic knowledge is only 10 percent. The skills that will make the difference between Michael's past life of quiet desperation and his current life, securing and using the keys to success, are not his technical skills alone, but his mastery of soft (life) skills.

But there is a word of warning. When you find a willing mentor/coach, demonstrate your appreciation by following his or her advice and being a committed learner as Michael demonstrates to Charlie.

It will take courage to leave your comfort zone, but the rewards will be with you for a lifetime. Observe the change in you, your attitude, your beliefs, and your successes; you won't go back.

The questions to ask yourself are simple: Are these people like me? Do my friends, family, and business associates inspire, motivate, teach, and demonstrate through their actions that I can achieve and be more than I am or think I can be? Do they expect more from me? Do they believe in me? Do I demonstrate that I am worthy of their coaching?

CRITICAL OUTCOMES FOR PILLAR SIX:
- Recognizing the influence others have on our lives
- Choosing positive and supportive relationships
- Identifying and developing mentor relationships

IDENTIFYING ROLE MODELS AND POSITIVE ASSOCIATIONS

Relationships are a critical part of success. In **Twelve Pillars**, Charlie challenges Michael to look at whom he associates with and the influence those individuals have on his life. Purely by accident, Michael has now stumbled upon a very positive influence in his life, namely Charlie. This story demonstrates the power of mentoring.

In this activity, reflect on one or two individuals who have served as positive role models or mentors in your personal or professional life. They may be a long-time trusted friend, a current or former supervisor or work colleague, a parent or relative, perhaps a teacher, coach, or community leader.

1. Name of my Mentor or Role Model: _____

2. What qualities does this person possess that I admire?
   _____
   _____

3. What messages do this person's attitudes and actions convey to me?
   _____
   _____

4. Have I talked with this person about my Long-Range Goals?
   _____
   _____

5. How can this person assist me in reaching those goals?
   _____
   _____
   _____
   _____

MISTAKES TO AVOID

As you use this workbook, you will find activities that help you focus on developing those skills. You will also have opportunities to reflect on behaviors that may keep you from achieving the level of success for which you strive.

Which one of these **Mistakes to Avoid** is the one you need to work on changing in your life?

Skill: Optimism/Positive Attitude and Ambition

- **Surrounding yourself with negative, depressing, and pessimistic people.** Result: Become like those with whom you associate, their attitudes infecting you like a contagious disease.
- **Looking at life, situations, and events around you in a negative manner or as hopeless.** Result: Miss the golden opportunities and/or the greater lessons. Hopelessness can be a state of mind and not a state of your circumstances.
- **Maintaining a bad attitude without a desire to improve or contribute to improving conditions or circumstances.** Result: Impart doom and gloom to those around you. Become part of the problem and not part of the solution. Live in a constant state of despair, misery, loneliness, and isolation.
- **Your words are positive, but your actions are negative or destructive.** Result: Your actions are so loud no one can hear your words.

Skill: Observation

- **Forming fixed judgments of others based upon singular events.** Result: Make snap judgments about others; allow no quarter for human weaknesses or lapses in judgment. Trust that your abilities will spare you from becoming the object of similar snap judgments.
- **Discontinuing observations before validating or confirming conclusions.** Result: Assume that the pool is full because the diving board is in place. Pray you are correct as you leap to your conclusion.
- **Believing there is nothing you can learn by observing others.** Result: Disregard the fact that most of what you have learned has been through observing others. Remain firm in your resolve to make your own mistakes.
- **Accepting theories posed by others as factual without making or considering your own observations.** Result: Inspire others to pose a theory that you are naïve, gullible, or terribly lazy. Respond to this theory accordingly.

EVALUATING YOUR ASSOCIATIONS

We are indeed known, and influenced, by the company we keep. In the following article, Jim Rohn (co-author of **Twelve Pillars**) suggests ways to analyze whom we associate with and why. Read the short narrative and then answer the reflective questions that follow.

If you were to evaluate the major influences in your life that have shaped the kind of person you are, this has to be high on the list: the people and thoughts you choose to allow into your life. Mr. Shoaff (Jim's mentor) gave me a very important warning in those early days that I would like to share with you. He said, "Never underestimate the power of influence." Indeed, the influence of those around us is so powerful! Many times we don't even realize we're being strongly affected because influences generally develop over an extended period of time.

Peer pressure is an especially powerful force because it is so subtle. If you're around people who spend all they make, chances are excellent that you'll spend all you make. If you are around people who go to more ball games than concerts, chances are excellent that you'll do the same thing. If you are around people who don't read, chances are excellent that you won't read. People can keep nudging us off course a little at a time until finally, we find ourselves asking, "How did I get here?" Those subtle influences need to be studied carefully if we really want our lives to turn out the way we've planned.

With regard to this important point, let me give you three key questions to ask yourself. They may help you to make better analysis of your current associations.

Here is the first question: "Who am I around?" Make a mental note of the people with whom you most often associate. You've got to evaluate everybody who is able to influence you in any way.

The second question is: "What are these associations doing to me?" That's a major question to ask. What have they got me doing? What have they got me listening to? What have they got me reading? Where have they got me going? What do they have me thinking? How have they got me talking? How have they got me feeling? What have they got me saying? You've got to make a serious study of how others are influencing you, both negatively and positively.

Here's a final question: "Is that okay?" Maybe everyone you associate with has been a positive, energizing influence. Then again, maybe there are some bad apples in the bunch. All I'm suggesting here is that you take a close and objective look. Everything is worth a second look, especially the power of influence. Both will take you somewhere, but only one will take you in the direction you need to go.

It's easy to just dismiss the things that influence our lives. One man say's, "I live here, but I don't think it matters. I'm around these people, but I don't think it hurts." I would take another look at that. Remember, everything matters! Sure, some things matter more than others, but everything amounts to something. You've got to keep checking to find out whether your associations are tipping the scales toward the positive or toward the negative. Ignorance is never the best policy. Finding out is the best policy.

Perhaps you've heard the story of the little bird. He had his wing over his eye and he was crying. The owl said to the bird, "You are crying." "Yes," said the little bird, and he pulled his wing away from his eye. "Oh, I see," said the owl. "You're crying because the big bird pecked out your eye." And the little bird said, "No, I'm not crying because the big bird pecked out my eye. I'm crying because I let him."

It's easy to let influence shape our lives, to let associations determine our direction, to let pressures overwhelm us, and to let tides take us. The big question is, are we letting ourselves become what we wish to become?

(by Jim Rohn)

1. "Never underestimate the power of influence." Name the person who has had the most influence on your life. Has that influence been positive or negative?

   _____

   _____

2. Mentors play an important role in our lives. In **Twelve Pillars**, Charlie has become a mentor to Michael, and in this narrative, Jim refers to "Mr. Shoaff," a person who has had a tremendous influence on his personal and professional development for many years. Have you ever had a mentor or been one to someone else? What did each of you get from that relationship?

   _____

   _____

INFLUENCES IN OUR LIVES

In the article "Evaluating Your Associations," Jim Rohn asks three questions about the people with whom we associate. In the chart below, reflect on your family, friends, and business associates, and consider how their relationships with you are influencing your life.

Who am I around?	What are these associations doing to me?	Is that okay?

Reviewing the chart, consider the influences others have on you.

1. Are you satisfied with what is on this chart?
   _____
   _____

2. What changes, if any, do you think need to be made?
   _____
   _____

OBSERVING PATTERNS OF BEHAVIOR

Much of what we learn in life results directly from our ability to observe. There is a wealth of knowledge to be gained by observing people and the world around us. That wealth of knowledge is gained via our ability to observe with a purpose – to learn and to understand.

Observation also serves as an early detection and warning system that enables us to recognize and respond appropriately to both subtle and dramatic changes, alerting us equally to promises of danger or delight. Observation is not limited to one sense, but integrates data from all sensory input, providing us critical information, even in the absence of one or more senses.

Although each of us possesses the capacity to observe, highly successful people do it constantly. From reading books to studying people, processes, and systems, these observant individuals are able to capture the complete picture along with all essential details. They learn from what others do and gain insight into why they do it. With practice and consistent use of information gathered from observing, they are able to predict outcomes in most circumstances, and make sound decisions as a result.

People are creatures of habit. Observe individuals and you will be able to predict and anticipate responses, behaviors, and attitudes with some degree of accuracy. Often, these observations can lead us to make character, behavior, and attitude changes in ourselves when we see ourselves in others.

Reflect on the following **Steps to Successful Observation** and consider how observant you are about the people around you.

Exercise heightened awareness of what you perceive through your senses of sight, hearing, smell, touch, and taste.

- What senses do you use most frequently to obtain information?
- Which do you use the least?
- How can you employ your other senses, including your "sixth sense" of intuition, to observe your surroundings in new and better ways?

Apply the knowledge you have gained through your life and academic experiences to improve your observation skills.

- What have you learned in the past that can help you improve your skills of observation?
- What academic courses did you take that emphasized critical observation? These might include the sciences, sociology, graphic arts, history and art appreciation, literary analysis clinical studies, statistics, or others.

- In what ways do these areas of knowledge and experience come together to help you understand and form conclusions about new experiences?

Observe others over sufficient time to identify patterns of behavior and attitude.

Choose a family member or friend to reflect on.

- Do you take the time to observe the way this person behaves in different situations?
- Do you resist the urge to judge this person based on isolated events?
- Do you focus on patterns of behavior rather than individual moments with this person?
- Do you allow for the possibility that we are all capable of good and poor judgment and variations in strength or weakness of character, depending on circumstances?
- Do you extend the benefit of the doubt to this person until sufficient evidence indicates otherwise?

MY LIST OF RELATIONSHIP GOALS

This chapter has focused on the tremendous influence others have on us – on our attitudes, our behaviors, and especially our opportunities for success in reaching our long-term goals. In **Twelve Pillars**, Charlie explains to Michael that every relationship is an association, and each association has a positive, neutral, or negative effect on him.

In the chart on the next page, do the following:

- Write down your Long-Range Goal in the space provided.
- Using the list from the previous activity, reflect on each person and determine how your relationship with them will support the achievement of your Long-Range Goal.
- Place each person into one of three categories: Disassociation, Limited Association, and Expanded Association.
- Create a short-term (six months or less) goal to address that relationship. If it is not in the Expanded Association category, you may determine that it is a relationship that can be changed. If that relationship is holding you back from achieving success, you may need to create a short-term goal that reduces or eliminates the time you spend with that person.

My Long-Range Goal: _____

DISASSOCIATION	**LIMITED ASSOCIATION**	**EXPANDED ASSOCIATION**
Person:	Person:	Person:
Goal:	Goal:	Goal:
Person:	Person:	Person:
Goal:	Goal:	Goal:
Person:	Person:	Person:
Goal:	Goal:	Goal:
Person:	Person:	Person:
Goal:	Goal:	Goal:
Person:	Person:	Person:
Goal:	Goal:	Goal:
Person:	Person:	Person:
Goal:	Goal:	Goal:
Person:	Person:	Person:
Goal:	Goal:	Goal:

Listed below are the Critical Skills needed to be proficient in this Pillar. Also listed are the Additional Essential Skills needed for mastery.

Critical Skills	Additional Essential Skills
Observation	Responsibility
Decision Making	Problem Solving
Accountability	Commitment
Project Planning/Goal Setting	Optimism/Positive Attitude and Ambition

Pillar Seven

"Formal education will earn you a living.
Self-education will make you a fortune."

Before you begin this portion of the **Twelve Pillars Workbook**, read or reread Chapter 7, *Be a Life-Long Learner,* of **Twelve Pillars**.

Pillar Seven

"There are a few mainstays to learning that anyone can use to improve their lives. The first is to read books. The second is to learn from successful people by observation. And the third is to constantly reflect on your own experiences and learn what went right and what went wrong." (Charlie, **Twelve Pillars**)

Self-education involves reading, observing, and reflecting. As you consider your life-long learning plan, all three should be central elements. You may have spent a long time in formal educational settings or you may not have finished high school. What matters is what you choose to do from this point forward to develop positive learning habits that will assist you in achieving all the goals in your life.

Reading with comprehension is essential to job performance and advancement in almost every field. Research shows that people who read literature on a regular basis generally earn higher incomes. Reading helps individuals develop more effective oral and written communication skills that strengthen relationships. Skilled readers research information to discern between unsubstantiated opinions and verifiable facts. These abilities increase learning, strengthen decisions, and build credibility with others.

In addition to reading, much of what we learn in life results directly from our ability to observe. There is a wealth of knowledge to be gained by observing people and the world around us. That wealth of knowledge is gained via our ability to observe with a purpose – to learn and to understand.

Although each of us possesses the capacity to observe, highly successful people do it constantly. From reading books to studying people, processes, and systems, these observant individuals are able to capture the complete picture along with all essential details. They learn from what others do and gain insight into why they do it. With practice and consistent use of information gathered from observing, they are able to predict successes and failures, accurately predict outcomes in most circumstances, and make sound decisions as a result.

CRITICAL OUTCOMES FOR PILLAR SEVEN:
- Developing positive reading and observation habits
- Cultivating an orientation to formal and informal life-long learning
- Setting goals which foster life-long learning practices

READING TO ENRICH YOUR LIFE

In **Twelve Pillars**, Charlie gives Michael a list of twenty books that he advises everyone should read. Use this page as a reference as you begin your life-long "reading education." Each time you come across a book that enriches your life, write it down here. In addition to jotting down Key Ideas, you may want to develop your "mentor" role by referring particular books to others.

TITLE:	
AUTHOR:	
DATE READ:	
KEY IDEAS:	
Someone I want to share this book with:	

TITLE:	
AUTHOR:	
DATE READ:	
KEY IDEAS:	
Someone I want to share this book with:	

TITLE:
AUTHOR:
DATE READ:
KEY IDEAS:
Someone I want to share this book with:

TITLE:
AUTHOR:
DATE READ:
KEY IDEAS:
Someone I want to share this book with:

TITLE:
AUTHOR:
DATE READ:
KEY IDEAS:
Someone I want to share this book with:

MISTAKES TO AVOID

As you use this workbook, you will find activities that help you focus on developing those skills. You will also have opportunities to reflect on behaviors that may keep you from achieving the level of success for which you strive.

Which one of these **Mistakes to Avoid** is the one you need to work on changing in your life?

Skill: Reading

- **Avoiding reading at all costs.** Result: Pay dearly. Foster ignorance, lose opportunities, and experience the slow but certain degeneration of your mind.

- **Using the television and computer as primary sources of information.** Result: Gain remote expertise, maximize mouse manipulation, and acquire sufficient but limited knowledge.

- **Believing everything you read.** Result: Find yourself lost in a sea of conflicting ideas with no compass to guide you and with confusion as your constant companion.

Skill: Observation

- **Thinking that you are too busy to observe what is happening around you.** Result: See yourself as a worker bee that must focus diligently to finish a task, taking no time to consider the bigger picture.

- **Disregarding observation as an effective personnel management tool.** Result: Fail to observe significant patterns of attitudes and behavior in others. Experience perpetual astonishment in their ability to surprise and amaze you in so many ways! Explain this phenomenon to your superiors when they question your ability to manage others.

- **Doubting there is anything you can learn by observing others.** Result: Disregard the fact that most of what you have learned has been through your eyes. Remain firm in your resolve to make your own mistakes.

Skill: Decision Making

- **Making decisions based only on emotions rather than including reliable data and information.** Result: Enjoy erratic and irrational decisions that will likely lead to poor outcomes.

- **Avoiding making decisions to prevent conflict or to please others.** Result: Impede progress, generate uncertainty, undermine confidence, and please no one.

- **Ignoring your gut instincts/internal compass.** Result: Lose your sense of direction and let the tide of chance carry you.

TEN THINGS I WISH I WOULD HAVE KNOWN

Being a life-long learner means learning from life. In the following article, Chris Widener (co-author of **Twelve Pillars**) reveals the ten things he wishes he'd learned, with the hope that you will learn from his experiences. Read the short narrative and then answer the reflective questions that follow.

I must confess, I laughed when I saw that Maria Shriver has come out with a book called, "Ten Things I Wish I Had Known Before Going Into The Real World." The real world? Come on, she grew up a Kennedy and married the biggest action movie star of all time! That aside, it got me to thinking: What are ten things I wish I would have known before going out into the real world? So, here they are...

Life isn't fair. *You know, your mother always told you this but as kids we never believe it. We think that somehow mom was two tacos short of a combo plate and that eventually we will go into the real world and show her how those who work hard and do right always do come out on top. Then after about five years we become disenchanted and start to smell the coffee. Life isn't fair! Why didn't anybody tell me that? I guess they did, didn't they? Unfortunately, sometimes the bad guys win. Sometimes people die early. We shouldn't take this lightly, but we must be realists. While we accept what comes our way, we still strive to work hard, dream big, and do right.*

People play favorites. *It is true that it isn't what you know but who you know that counts. This is because people play favorites. Sometimes it doesn't matter that you are the best person or have the lowest bid. People will regularly cut deals with people they like or who can scratch their back in return. I guess the lesson to learn is that while we strive to achieve much and have excellent skills, we should also develop a strong network of healthy relationships.*

People will let you down. *Being a person who does what he says can be a blessing and a curse. It is a blessing because I am able to look at myself in the mirror each day. It is a curse because if you are like that, you will most likely expect that from others and yet they will regularly let you down. People can be bad at keeping their word or doing what is right. I could have relieved a lot of emotional stress if I would have known this one before getting out into the real world.*

Not everybody wants to grow personally. *I just assumed that everybody loved to learn and to grow. I thought everybody wanted to get better at what they did. The reality is, however, that most people do not. That is why there is something that we call "average." Most people want to stay where they are. That is why they do. Those who strive to go forward will always be cutting against the grain and will often be resented, even if quietly, for it.*

The stock market goes down sometimes. *Some of you older folks knew this. But us young whippersnappers, we have been riding it high on the hog for a while. This is good in a sense, but unless you have some common sense of how financial markets work, you can get quite a shock from time to time. You see, before you get into the real world, everything gets handed to you and you* really don't have to work for much. Then you do and you think that every investment will turn out grand – whoops!

The older you get, the harder it is to lose weight. I was always a little "pudgy." Nothing big, just not like the cover guys of Men's Health Magazine (You know, the ones that say "Six-pack abs in 20 minutes a day." I think that means they only eat twenty minutes a day, and it is usually stewed vegetables! But I digress…). If I would have known better, I would have worked harder when I was younger to keep the weight off so I wouldn't have to work that much harder now!

Marriage is work. A good marriage is more work. When you are young you think, "I'll find the girl of my dreams and we'll live happily ever after." Well, hello! You forget that your spouse is human and you are too, most of the time! To live under the same roof with someone and to work out likes and dislikes, personalities, and schedules, not to mention life goals and the like is HARD WORK! Not drudgery, just work. Yes, there will be plenty of bliss and joy, but marriage will make you work for it!

It takes longer to get out of debt than to get into it. I have never really had much debt. I did take out student loans to pay for school and wow, do they take a long time to get out of. Fortunately I have them paid off but for a while there, it was one of the big checks we wrote every month. Many people think credit cards are great because they can have what they want when they want it. Too bad they don't realize that twenty minutes of shopping ecstasy will result in months or years of payments.

It doesn't work to try to please others. I have always wanted people to like me. Many times, I wanted them to like me too much. That isn't good. This doesn't work because I realized that most of the time, people liking or disliking you has nothing to do whatsoever with rational thought. Some people will dislike you, no matter how well you have done, and others will love you, warts and all. So I do my best and let the chips fall where they may – now.

You need to tend to your spiritual, emotional, and physical health or you will crash hard. If you don't take time for yourself, both inwardly and outwardly, your body will catch up with you. You can take time for yourself by choice or not. It is much more fun by choice! Life is hard and it can and will weigh you down. We need to tend the fires of spirit and mind while keeping our physical bodies tuned for success as well. If not, our bodies break down.

Bonus: In spite of the above, life is very much worth it! Some of the above may seem like bummers. They aren't the "positive" things we like to focus on, but they are true. Being positive doesn't mean sticking your head in the ground in order to avoid the negative of life. What it means is that we are realists who understand the negative aspects of life and choose to be optimists instead. We deal with the negative and pursue the positive. That is why I can say that life is worth living no matter how expensive or painful the lessons I have had to learn have been. Life is good and I can make it better!

So I had to learn some lessons AFTER I got into the real world. So what? At least I learned them and can live the rest of my life to the fullest from now on! I hope you can too!

(by Chris Widener)

One of the ways Charlie advised Michael to continue his life-long learning was through constant reflection. While you have had many opportunities to do that already in this workbook, let's practice going into more depth by reflecting on this article.

1. Choose one of the "lessons" that impressed you the most and write it here:

   _____
   _____
   _____

2. What was your initial reaction when you first read it?

   _____
   _____
   _____

3. Describe a personal experience you or someone you know had that relates to this "lesson."

   _____
   _____
   _____

4. Now think about the Long-Range Goal and other changes you are making in your life. How might this lesson apply?

   _____
   _____
   _____

5. As you are learning new concepts and applying them to your own life, you also have the opportunity to serve as a mentor to others and pass that knowledge on. With whom could you share this lesson? How could you go about doing that?

   _____
   _____
   _____

MY LIST OF GOALS – LIFE-LONG LEARNING

You have spent a great deal of time focusing on your Long-Range Goal, setting smaller Mid-Range and Short-Term Goals. Have you included goals that ensure you will continue good life-long learning habits? If not, create at least one in the space below.

1. _____

2. _____

3. _____

Listed below are the Critical Skills needed to be proficient in this Pillar. Also listed are the Additional Essential Skills needed for mastery.

Critical Skills	Additional Essential Skills
Personal Development/Self-Improvement	Commitment
Reading	Honesty/Integrity
Observation	Loyalty
Decision Making	Finances

Pillar Eight

"One key to having influence with others is to have others perceive you as a person of talent and virtue."

Before you begin this portion of the **Twelve Pillars Workbook**, read or reread Chapter 8, *All of Life is Sales*, of **Twelve Pillars**.

Pillar Eight

"You cannot speak that which you do not know. You cannot translate that which you do not have. And you cannot give that which you do not possess. To give it and share it, and for it to be effective, you first need to have it. If you are going to sell a product you have to know it, believe in it, and feel it. And the same is true if you are selling yourself." (Charlie, **Twelve Pillars**)

Being perceived as a person of talent and virtue is not necessarily an easy task. Yet it is essential that each of us strives for those qualities if we want to be successful and achieve the goals we have set for ourselves. In **Twelve Pillars**, Charlie explains that talent and virtue are often the same as skill and character. At the heart of a strong character lie honesty and integrity.

These character traits cannot be situational. To have integrity and to be honest requires a commitment to full-time practice in all circumstances, not just when it's convenient or self-serving to do so. Situational integrity and selective honesty are disingenuous and dishonest at their core.

What does this look like in our daily lives? It means that we are truthful and sincere in all of our dealings with others, whether personal or professional. We choose to be scrupulous in all we do, resisting temptations to lie, cheat, or steal, instead pursuing what is right, even when it is uncomfortable, goes against popular opinion, or is costly.

Why should we be persons of talent and virtue, practicing honesty and integrity? Life is unpredictable. Sometimes unplanned or catastrophic events occur, leaving financial troubles in its wake. All that may be left is your reputation, the relationships you've established, and the knowledge you've gained. At these times, a reputation founded on honesty and integrity will enable you to recover. Your friends and associates will support and help you through it; they'll open doors of opportunity.

CRITICAL OUTCOMES FOR PILLAR EIGHT:
- Identifying the steps to successful honesty/integrity
- Creating strategies to achieve influence

BECOMING A PERSON OF TALENT AND VIRTUE

In **Twelve Pillars**, Charlie advises Michael to become a "better influencer." He goes on to explain: "The key to influencing others is to have others perceive you as a person of talent and virtue. . . (which are) the same as character and skill. Be a person of strong character and increasing skill and you will always be growing in your influence."

Consider your own level of influence and how you are perceived by others. Read and reflect on the following Steps to Success. If you choose to, write your thoughts on one or more Steps in the space provided on the pages following this activity.

1. **Tell the truth and adhere to the facts. Never intentionally lie or mislead yourself or others.** Reflect on a recent interaction with another person (supervisor, colleague, spouse, friend, neighbor) and ask yourself the following questions:
   - *Did I gather all the relevant facts before responding?*
   - *Was I honest in my interpretation of the situation?*
   - *Was I honest in presenting those facts to other concerned parties?*
   - *Did I try to reinvent or skew the facts to place others or myself in a better light?*
   - *Did I withhold or obscure information to soften the blow or minimize the situation?*
   - *Did I speak the truth despite possible consequences?*

2. **Be truthful, sincere, and straightforward in dealing with others.** Reflect on an ongoing relationship with another person and ask yourself these questions:
   - *Am I truthful and sincere in my interactions with this person?*
   - *Do I refrain from speaking when I cannot speak the truth without causing unnecessary harm to him/her?*
   - *Do my words reflect my thoughts?*
   - *Do my actions support my words?*
   - *Do I respect this person enough to deal with him/her honestly and fairly?*

3. **Act consistently in ways that prove you are trustworthy and honorable.** Reflect on your daily behaviors in your workplace and at home and consider the following questions:

    - *Do I let my actions speak for me, or do I insist on verbalizing my own credentials? (Translation – Do I walk the walk or just talk the talk?)*
    - *Am I trustworthy in all that I do?*
    - *Are my motives consistently honorable?*
    - *Do I challenge myself when I suspect that my motives are less than worthy, or do I attempt to deceive others and myself into believing otherwise?*
    - *Do I consult a trusted advisor when my actions and motives are unclear?*

4. **Build relationships on a foundation of honesty and integrity.** Reflect on a new relationship and consider the following questions:

    - *Do I value this relationship enough to commit to complete honesty and integrity?*
    - *Will I examine my attitudes, words, and actions through the lens of this commitment?*
    - *When in doubt, will I opt to do the honorable thing?*
    - *What part of this relationship will I be willing to risk if I were to break trust with this person?*
    - *How would I feel and what would I do if this person ever broke trust with me?*

REFLECTIONS ON MY STEPS TO SUCCESS

MISTAKES TO AVOID

As you use this workbook, you will find activities that help you focus on developing those skills. You will also have opportunities to reflect on behaviors that may keep you from achieving the level of success for which you strive.

Which one of these **Mistakes to Avoid** is the one you need to work on changing in your life?

Skill: Honesty/Integrity

- **Practicing honesty and integrity when it is convenient or necessary to impress others.** Result: Pretend you are someone you are not. Discard these character traits like changeable costumes and then find yourself revealed.
- **Justifying your dishonest behavior with the belief that everyone else does the same thing.** Result: Learn that significant others (such as your boss, your spouse or your children, your friends and associates) do not ascribe to the same belief.
- **Pursuing short-term gain at the risk of long-term pain.** Result: You will receive all that you give, good or bad, at some time in your life. You may get away with it today, but you will be discovered and pay a price for it later.

Skill: Leadership

- **Believing that rules and their enforcement constitute leadership.** Result: Create a forced following that operates on fear and is completely devoid of trust, respect, and creativity. Demotivated and disloyal employees, friends, or family members.
- **Misusing or abusing your position, power, or the trust others place in you.** Result: Hurt others, damage the organization, and, ultimately, lose all that has true and lasting value.
- **Showing little or no respect for those impacted by your decisions and choices.** Result: What you give you shall receive in abundance – in all things good or bad.

Skill: Respect

- **Attempting to appear respectful to misuse, or manipulate others.** Result: Live a life based on lies. Make every attempt to keep your façade intact, but expect that the truth will prevail, in some way and at some time, to the demise of your artificial image and falsely premised relationships.
- **Operating from a foundation of poor or nonexistent self-respect.** Result: Find that you cannot build genuine respect for others – or earn their respect – from a weak foundation. Continue to live in a way that deprives you of meaningful and rewarding relationships and opportunities.

MAINTAINING HONESTY AND INTEGRITY

In the following article, Jim Rohn (co-author of **Twelve Pillars**) considers how daily behaviors speak volumes about the character and integrity of a person. Read the short narrative and then answer the reflective questions that follow.

For a leader, honesty and integrity are absolutely essential to survival. A lot of business people don't realize how closely they're being watched by their subordinates. Remember when you were a kid in grammar school, how you used to sit there staring at your teacher all day? By the end of the school year, you could do a perfect imitation of all your teacher's mannerisms. You were aware of the slightest nuances in your teacher's voice - all the little clues that distinguished levels of meaning that told you the difference between bluff and "now I mean business".

And you were able to do that after eight or nine months of observation. Suppose you had five or 10 years. Do you think there would have been anything about your teacher you didn't know?

Now fast forward and use that analogy as a manager. Do you think there's anything your people don't know about you right this minute? If you haven't been totally aboveboard and honest with them, do you really think you've gotten away with it? Not too likely. But if you've been led to believe that you've gotten away with it, there might be a good probability that people are afraid of you, and that's a problem in its own right.

But there is another side of this coin. In any organization, people want to believe in their leaders. If you give them reason to trust you, they're not going to go looking for reasons to think otherwise, and they'll be just as perceptive about your positive qualities as they are about the negative ones.

A situation that happened some years ago at a company in the Midwest illustrates this perfectly. The wife of a new employee experienced complications in the delivery of a baby. There was a medical bill of more than $10,000, and the health insurance company didn't want to cover it. The employee hadn't been on the payroll long enough, the pregnancy was a preexisting condition, etc, etc,..

In any case, the employee was desperate. He approached the company CEO and asked him to talk to the insurance people. The CEO agreed, and the next thing the employee knew, the bill was gone and the charges were rescinded. Then he told some colleagues about the way the CEO had so readily used his influence with the insurance company, they just shook their heads and smiled. The CEO had paid the bill out of his own pocket, and everybody knew it, no matter how quietly it had been done.

Now an act of dishonesty can't be hidden either, and it will instantly undermine the authority of a leader. But an act of integrity and kindness like the example above is just as obvious to all concerned. When you're in a leadership position, you have the choice of how you will be seen. You will be seen one way or the other, make no mistake about it.

One of the most challenging areas of leadership is your family. Leadership of a family demands even higher standards of honesty and integrity, and the stakes are higher too. You can replace disgruntled employees and start over. You can even get a new job for yourself, if it comes to that. But your family can't be shuffled like a deck of cards. If you haven't noticed, kids are great moral philosophers, especially as they get into adolescence. They're determined to discover and expose any kind of hypocrisy, phoniness, or lack of integrity on the part of authority figures, and if we're parents, that means us. It's frightening how unforgiving kids can be about this, but it really isn't a conscious decision on their part; it's just a necessary phase of growing up. They're testing everything, especially their parents.

As a person of integrity yourself, you'll find it easy to teach integrity to your kids, and they in turn will find it easy to accept you as a teacher. This is a great opportunity and also a supreme responsibility, because kids simply must be taught to tell the truth: to mean what they say and to say what they mean.

"Praise is one the world's most effective teaching and leadership tools. Criticism and blame, even if deserved, are counter productive unless all other approaches have failed."

Now for the other side of the equation, we all know people who have gotten ahead as a result of dishonest or unethical behavior. When you're a kid, you might naively think that never happens, but when you get older, you realize that it does. Then you think you've really wised up. But that's not the real end of it. When you get older, you see the long-term consequences of dishonest gain, and you realize that in the end it doesn't pay.

"Hope of dishonest gain is the beginning of loss". I don't think that old saying refers to loss of money. I think it actually means loss of self-respect. You can have all the material things in the world, but if you've lost respect for yourself, what do you really have? The only way to ever attain success and enjoy it is to achieve it honestly with pride in what you've done.

(by Jim Rohn)

1. "Actions speak louder than words." Consider how this saying sums up the message in Jim's narrative. Describe a recent situation in your workplace that comes to mind as an example of this – it may be something a supervisor or colleague did, or something you did yourself.

   _____

   _____

2. What was the "message" being conveyed through those actions?

   _____

   _____

3. Jim makes the statement that "Praise is one of the world's most effective teaching and leadership tools." When was the last time you praised someone? Describe the experience.

   _____
   _____

4. How did you feel?

   _____
   _____

   How did the person you praised respond to you?

   _____
   _____

5. "Hope of dishonest gain is the beginning of loss." Jim suggests that his is more than just a loss of money, but rather a loss of self-respect. What are your thoughts about this statement?

   _____
   _____

SELLING YOURSELF

In **Twelve Pillars**, Charlie advises Michael to "know your stuff." This means talking to lots of people and never taking "no" for an answer. This applies not only to successful sales, but to achieving long-range and short-term goals.

In the space below, list ten people you will talk to in the next week about your goals and how they might help you achieve them. Next to each name, jot some notes about what you want to talk with them about specifically.

WHO I WANT TO TALK WITH   **WHAT I WANT TO TALK ABOUT**

1. _____   _____
2. _____   _____
3. _____   _____
4. _____   _____
5. _____   _____
6. _____   _____
7. _____   _____
8. _____   _____
9. _____   _____
10. _____   _____

Listed below are the Critical Skills needed to be proficient in this Pillar. Also listed are the Additional Essential Skills needed for mastery.

Critical Skills	Additional Essential Skills
Honesty/Integrity	Accountability
Leadership	Responsibility
Respect	Trust

Pillar Nine

"What you become directly influences what you get."

Before you begin this portion of the **Twelve Pillars Workbook**, read or reread Chapter 9, *Income Seldom Exceeds Personal Development*, of **Twelve Pillars**.

Pillar Nine

*Anything of significance is going to be hard, Michael. You may as well accept that. Remember: The Pain of Discipline or the Pain of Regret. Your choice."
(Charlie, **Twelve Pillars**)*

In our current economy, we not only accept debt, we also expect debt. Powerful images and well-contrived messages seduce us into believing that spending and acquiring will lead to happiness and contentment. Our mailboxes overflow with offers of "easy" money, promising to deliver a richer lifestyle before we have earned it. The tantalizing dreams are depicted with bold, colorful images and large print – the terms of potential enslavement to debt are not. We have unwittingly bought into a concept promoted by those who stand to gain from our reckless spending, need for instant gratification, and "feel-good" mentality.

The universal use of credit and debit cards has replaced cash transactions. Each swipe of our magnified strip enters our personal credit information into large computerized databases. Despite efforts to protect consumers, these systems are not foolproof and put us at great risk for identity theft and fraud. Caution, discretion, and regular monitoring of our credit statements and reports are essential to our financial security.

Successful money management demands constant attention, self-discipline, and constructive habits. At a minimum, we must 1) acquire a basic but clear understanding of finances and learn how to make our money work for us; 2) conduct thoughtful and thorough financial planning; 3) commit to a budget that is well within our means; 4) implement disciplined savings and wise investing; 5) build in allowances and contingencies for income shifts, losses, or emergencies; 6) avoid all unnecessary debt; 7) diligently protect our personal financial information and reputation; and 8) differentiate between want and need.

CRITICAL OUTCOMES FOR PILLAR NINE:

- Creating and managing a financial budget
- Setting goals for true wealth

TRACKING YOUR MONEY

In **Twelve Pillars**, Charlie tells Michael that anything that has importance in life will be hard. He called it "The Pain of Discipline or the Pain of Regret." Making wise financial decisions begins with an understanding of what you spend your money on, how you make those choices, and the consequences of those decisions.

In the following activity, begin by thinking about where your money goes each day. Use the log on the next page over a three-day period to record every cent you spend (cash or credit), what you spend it on, and why you made that choice. NOTE: Try not to pick a time period where you pay all the household bills. The log should reflect a typical spending pattern in your life.

TRACKING YOUR MONEY — LOG

Record your expenses here during a three-day period. You don't need to write every single item down under Purchases if it is Groceries or some other multiple-item purchase. Leave the last column blank for now. Make additional copies as needed.

Date	Amount	Purchase*	Why?	+/-

MAKING DECISIONS ABOUT SPENDING

In the last activity, you recorded your spending over a typical three-day period. As you read back through the log to analyze your spending patterns, respond to the following questions:

1. **Essential Needs** – Consider which items on your list would be Essential Needs – that is, basic items you cannot live without. List them here, and indicate how much in total you spent on Essential Needs.

   _____
   _____
   _____
   _____
   _____
   _____

   Total on Essential Needs: _____

2. **Essential Wants** – Sometimes there are items we spend money on that are not required for basic needs, but are things that make our lives enjoyable. These might include a personal treat for you or for others, a special event or outfit, or something for which you've been saving and planning over a period of time. List any Essential Wants you spent money on and indicate the total below.

   _____
   _____
   _____
   _____
   _____
   _____

   Total on Essential Wants: _____

   How does this amount compare with the amount spent on Essential Needs? Is there a balance?

   _____

3. Charlie described the choices in spending as the Pain of Discipline and the Pain of Regret. Consider each of your purchases over the last three days and the reasons why you spend money on those items. Ask, "Is this item or service necessary? What would happen if I chose to live without it?"

4. On the right-hand side of the Log is a column labeled "+/-". Mark each spending decision that was Disciplined and positive with a **+** and indicate the ones that you regret or were poor choices with a **–**. Tally your **+** and **–** and record the totals below:

    Total +: _____   Total –: _____

    How do you feel about your spending for this period?
    _____
    _____

BUILDING A PERSONAL BUDGET

Building personal wealth begins with making positive financial choices and establishing discipline in spending habits. In the last activity, you focused on present behaviors and began reflecting on how those choices affect your long-term financial goals. In this activity, you will begin planning your spending for the future.

Budget worksheets are readily available from a variety of sources, including the Internet. A quick search of websites will bring up many templates and styles from which to choose. Using one of those formats or the one on the following page, identify your income and expenses on a monthly and annual basis. Determine what percentage of your income is being spent on Routine and Variable Expenses.

After you complete your first draft, review the following questions:

- Have I included all essential expenses, such as short- and long-term savings, food, household items, personal care, clothing, insurance, utilities, transportation costs, tuition, or medical and dental expenses?
- Have I considered additional expenses, such as hobbies and entertainment?
- Do my calculations accurately reflect my expenditures?
- Is this budget realistic?
- Is my income sufficient for this budget?
- If not, are there areas of spending I can reduce or eliminate?
- Have I allowed for irregularities that are associated with commission-based or self-employment income?
- How will I track and remain accountable for my spending?
- Have I separated Wants from Needs?

Personal Household Budget

	Date:		
Income	Monthly Amount	Yearly Amount (mth. x 12)	Percent
Net pay			
Second Job - Net Pay			
Investments			
Interest			
Other			
Total income			100.00%
Routine (or Fixed) Expenses	Monthly Amount	Yearly Amount (mth. x 12)	Percent
Rent or mortgage			
Car payments			
Child care			
Credit card payments			
Insurance (health, life and property)			
Telephone			
Utilities			
Other			
Total routine expenses			100.00%
Variable Expenses	Monthly Amount	Yearly Amount (mth. x 12)	Percent
Food			
Transportation (incl. gas, maintenance, parking, & taxis)			
Clothing (Purchases, Dry Cleaning)			
Education			
Entertainment			
Medication, Medical Visits, Glasses/Contacts			
Savings			
Other			
Total variable expenses			100.00%
Total monthly fixed and variable expenses			$0
Difference between monthly income and expenses: surplus / (deficit)			$0

MISTAKES TO AVOID

As you use this workbook, you will find activities that help you focus on developing those skills. You will also have opportunities to reflect on behaviors that may keep you from achieving the level of success for which you strive.

Which one of these **Mistakes to Avoid** is the one you need to work on changing in your life?

Skill: Decision Making

- **Making rash, impulsive decisions without considering potential short- and long-term consequences.** Result: Short-term gain, long-term pain.
- **Considering only your needs or desires in making a decision and ignore the needs of others.** Result: Be considered thoughtless, selfish, and inconsiderate.
- **Refusing to ask for guidance, input, or advice.** Result: Increase your chances of making a poor decision.

Skill: Finances

- **Perceiving wants as needs.** Result: Continue paying the debt long after the value of your prized acquisitions has depreciated. Lack required funds for essential needs or emergencies when they arise.
- **Delaying financial planning until a more convenient time.** Result: Avoid work and inconvenience today at the risk of financial troubles tomorrow. Lose income growth opportunities offered by timely and strategic investments. Allow financial challenges to become disasters as resources dwindle.
- **Developing a showcase budget and financial plan. Proceed to admire and ignore it simultaneously.** Result: Set the standard and then set yourself to the task of undermining it completely. Feel confounded by your lack of financial progress despite your plan. Install a first-rate financial security system, then ignore or disable the alarm.

Skill: Responsibility

- **Letting the fear of failure keep you from taking responsibility.** Result: Risk nothing and gain nothing. Deny yourself a better, more meaningful life.
- **Accepting responsibility without first determining whether you have the knowledge, skills, or abilities to carry it through.** Result: This is foolish. You will be resented if poor results negatively impact others.
- **Allowing pride to keep you from seeking assistance when you realize you cannot meet your responsibilities.** Result: Needing help is not a weakness unless you ask for help, receive it, and don't learn from it. Every accomplished man or woman has achieved success with help from others; failure is certainty if you insist on going it alone.

WHY GET RICH WHEN YOU CAN BE WEALTHY?

In the following article, Chris Widener (co-author of **Twelve Pillars**) reflects on the advantages of striving to be wealthy in all aspects of life. Read the short narrative and then answer the reflective questions that follow.

"Any fool can get rich, the wise get wealthy."

Getting rich is the main goal for a lot of people. That is unfortunate however, because there is something so much greater than simply the accumulation of money. Now don't get me wrong – I am not saying people shouldn't have large sums of money. In fact, I believe greatly in the power of money for good when in the hands of the right people. I think money is simply a tool that people can use to do great things – or bad things.

What is unfortunate is that so many people give up so much else in life in order to get those large sums of money. First of all, let me explain my quote about rich fools. Just turn on the TV or read a popular magazine and you will find lots of rich fools. You will see people with tons of money but who have no happiness, have drug problems and who leave behind them a string of broken relationships. These people are rich, not wealthy.

Rich people are people with lots of money. Wealthy people are people who are rich in life. This would include financial stability and freedom, but goes deeper into spiritual health, emotional and relational health, and of course physical health.

I think getting rich is easy. It is simply a discipline that anyone can do if they so choose. There are many examples of people who have made very little money who have left vast fortunes. Spend less than you earn, save more than you spend. Put what you spend into an interest bearing investment. Do this over a long period of time and you will get rich.

Wealthy? That is something altogether different. I have found that in most cases you must give up some wealth to get the riches. I know many rich people and very few of them are people who I would call wealthy. Most of them sacrificed their families, their health or their relationships as they pursued the accumulation of riches. The fact is that it takes time to make money. And every moment of time you spend in the pursuit of money is a moment of time taken from something else that would make you wealthy in life.

So let me ask you: Are you on the fast track toward riches? Or are you on the long-track toward true wealth?

Are you being wise with your finances so as to secure long-term financial stability and independence? I hope so, because that is certainly a part of being wealthy.

Are you investing in those closest to you? I hope so! The fact is that when you lay on your deathbed, it won't matter how much money you have. The grim reaper doesn't need any more money and so he can't be bought with yours! The only thing that will matter are those faces that surround you, the looks of love they give you, and the memories you have of good times spent with them.

Are you taking good care of yourself physically? I hope so because if you don't, you won't get the mileage out of it that you were intended too! Physical health is part of being wealthy!

Are you taking care of your spiritual life? I hope so because I don't think there are any more important questions we can answer than those whose answers will play themselves out for eternity. In my mind, spiritual questions make all the others seem like child's play. Are you taking good care of yourself emotionally? I hope so because it is your internal state that will give you the energy you are looking for to live long and the peace to enjoy that life of yours.

All in all, I have decided that I don't want to stoop to being rich. That is too low of a goal for me. I want to be wealthy – financially yes, but not to the exclusion of my body, soul and spirit. Not to the exclusion of deep and meaningful relationships with my friends and family. How about you? Will you be rich or wealthy?

(by Chris Widener)

1. "Wealthy people are people who are rich in life." What was your first reaction when you read that statement?

   _____

   _____

2. As you think about your life right now, are you on the "fast track toward riches" or "the long track toward true wealth?" Is that where you want to be? If not, what is the first thing you want to do to change?

   _____

   _____

3. Chris described four aspects of true wealth. On a scale of 1 (lowest) to 5 (highest), rate where you are right now in each of these areas as you move on the long track toward true wealth:

   Financial security _____

   Emotional / Relationships with others _____

   Physical health _____

   Spiritual health _____

GOAL SETTING FOR TRUE WEALTH

In Pillar Two, you listed the areas of your life you wanted to work on to improve body, mind, and spirit. All of these, along with financial goals, are aspects of Long-term true wealth. Review what you wrote in Chapter Two and update where you are on each of these goals in your life now.

The Body/Physical Health

What did I determine I would do to improve myself in this area?

_____

_____

On a scale of 1 to 5, with 5 meaning "I am using all my personal energy on this dimension" and 1 meaning "I am doing nothing at all," how would you rate your focus on this dimension now?   **1   2   3   4   5**

Set a goal for the next week for improving this aspect of long-term Wealth:

_____

_____

The Soul/Emotional Health/Relationships

What did I determine I would do to improve myself in this area?

On a scale of 1 to 5, with 5 meaning "I am using all my personal energy on this dimension" and 1 meaning "I am doing nothing at all," how would you rate your focus on this dimension now?   **1   2   3   4   5**

_____

_____

Set a goal for the next week for improving this aspect of long-term Wealth:

_____

_____

The Spirit/Spiritual Health

What did I determine I would do to improve myself in this area?

_____

_____

On a scale of 1 to 5, with 5 meaning "I am using all my personal energy on this dimension" and 1 meaning "I am doing nothing at all," how would you rate your focus on this dimension now? **1 2 3 4 5**

Set a goal for the next week for improving this aspect of long-term Wealth:

_____

_____

Financial Health

Review your budget and spending habits in earlier chapter activities.

What can I do to improve myself in this area?

_____

_____

On a scale of 1 to 5, with 5 meaning "I am using all my personal energy on this dimension" and 1 meaning "I am doing nothing at all," how would you rate your focus on this dimension now? **1 2 3 4 5**

Set a goal for the next week for improving this aspect of long-term Wealth:

_____

_____

Listed below are the Critical Skills needed to be proficient in this Pillar. Also listed are the Additional Essential Skills needed for mastery.

Critical Skills	Additional Essential Skills
Decision Making	Accountability
Finances	Fear and Anxiety
Responsibility	Prioritizing
Project Planning/Goal Setting	Team

Pillar Ten

"Communication is two or more people working together to find the common ground of understanding. And when they find that common ground, they are positioned to have tremendous power together."

Before you begin this portion of the **Twelve Pillars Workbook**, read or reread Chapter 10, *All Communication Brings the Common Ground of Understanding*, of **Twelve Pillars**.

Pillar Ten

"Mr. Davis always says, 'Communication isn't about what you say. It is also how you say it, when you say it, and the receptiveness of who you say it to. And that's just the half of it. The other half is making sure you really listen.'"
*(Charlie, **Twelve Pillars**)*

Effective listeners are rare and highly regarded assets to any organization and relationship. They not only hear what the speaker says, but also use cognitive, visual, and interpretive skills to engage with the speaker on multiple levels, interpreting both spoken and unspoken messages. Because there are many factors involved in verbal communications, effective listeners sustain focus, objectivity, and keen observation. At the same time, they demonstrate genuine respect for the speaker and interest in what the speaker has to say.

Often a speaker's postures, gestures, and features communicate more than his or her words. By observing body language, facial expressions, and speech patterns (voice volume and inflection, rate of speech, word choices, and continuity of thought) the effective listener grasps both the content and the context of what is said, allowing for more accurate interpretation. To accomplish this, the listener focuses on the speaker, sets aside preconceived notions and personal biases, and makes no assumptions about the speaker's intent. The good listener carefully follows the speaker, resisting the tendency to dwell on particular points, formulate responses, or drift into daydreams.

Skilled listeners meet the speaker's three basic human needs: 1) to like and to be liked; 2) to understand and to be understood; 3) to give and to receive. Attentive listening, open body language, and friendly or thoughtful expressions tell speakers he or she is liked and/or respected and that the audience is receptive. Asking appropriate questions tells the speaker listeners want to understand his or her intended message. Together, the speaker and listeners will find the common ground of understanding.

CRITICAL OUTCOMES FOR PILLAR TEN:

- Developing comprehensive listening skills
- Identifying the steps to successful negotiating strategies to reach agreement

DEVELOPING YOUR LISTENING TECHNIQUE

As Charlie explained to Michael in **Twelve Pillars**, the skill of listening is important, but what is more important is the character behind the skill. Real listening begins by focusing completely on the other person and valuing what he or she has to say. This skill takes practice. Attention focusing is a mental discipline. Just as you train your mind in meditation, relaxation, or martial arts, you are training your mind to take in information in all forms.

This activity requires a television or radio and about ten minutes of uninterrupted time on a regular basis. Try and practice this technique several times a week for the first few weeks until you become comfortable and confident in your abilities.

1. Choose a television or radio program where only one person is speaking for a continued period of time. Try a speech or lecture on a cable TV station or a public radio extended news report. Alternate this technique between TV and radio so you can work on both your visual and auditory listening skills.

2. Focus completely on the speaker. If you are watching a TV broadcast, listen to the words AND watch how the speaker acts. You may find that you begin thinking about other things fairly quickly. Each time your mind wanders, deliberately focus back on the speaker. Don't get discouraged if this keeps happening; focusing does get easier with practice.

3. Once you are able to focus on a speaker without distraction for at least ten minutes, you are ready to practice in the "real world." Try this technique in a lecture or sermon situation or in a business meeting and gain confidence in your skills as a "receiver of information" in a live setting.

MISTAKES TO AVOID

As you use this workbook, you will find activities that help you focus on developing those skills. You will also have opportunities to reflect on behaviors that may keep you from achieving the level of success for which you strive.

Which one of these **Mistakes to Avoid** is the one you need to work on changing in your life?

Skill: Listening

- **Staring blankly into space or think about something else while you are listening.** Result: At work, your chronic preoccupation will make the boss wonder whether you want to keep your job. At home, you will wonder why nobody ever tells you anything. With friends and acquaintances, you will just leave them wondering.
- **Interrupting the speaker needlessly.** Result: People will ignore or avoid you.

Skill: Observation

- **Believing there is nothing you can learn by observing others.** Result: Disregard that most of what you have learned has been through your eyes. Remain firm in your resolve to make your own mistakes when it's wise to learn from others.
- **Failing to confirm or validate your conclusions.** Result: Make incorrect assumptions and possibly poor choices or decisions as a result.

Skill: Respect

- **Treating others with the disdain and rudeness; embrace your sense of superiority.** Result: Some people will try to bring you down; others will avoid and ignore you. A pompous, righteous attitude denies you the opportunity to meet, enjoy, and befriend good people.
- **Attempting to build relationships in the absence of mutual respect.** Result: It won't work. Good relationships need a foundation of respect to succeed; without it they eventually fail.

Skill: Negotiating

- **Making little or no effort to identify the other party's significant needs.** Result: Aggravate the other party and lose the deal.
- **Setting up a "winner takes all" scenario.** Result: Break down negotiation processes and destroy trust and goodwill. No one likes to think they've lost.

THE SUBTLETY OF LANGUAGE

In the following article, Jim Rohn (co-author of **Twelve Pillars**) describes the power of language in achieving success. Read the short narrative and then answer the reflective questions that follow.

I have found that sometimes the subtle difference in our attitude, which of course can make a major difference in our future, can be as simple as the language we use. The difference in even how you talk to yourself or others. Consciously making a decision to quit saying what you don't want and to start saying what you do want. I call that faith. Believing the best, hoping for the best and moving toward the best.

A few examples could be, instead of saying "What if somebody doesn't respond" you start saying, "What if they do respond?" Instead of saying "What if someone says no?" You say, "What if they say yes?" Instead of "What if they start and quit?" say, "What if they start and stay?" or "What if it doesn't work out?" You say, "What if it does work out?" and the list goes on and on.

I found that when you start thinking and saying what you really want then your mind automatically shifts and pulls you in that direction. And sometimes it can be that simple, just a little twist in vocabulary that illustrates your attitude and philosophy.

Our language can also affect how others perform and behave around us. A teenager says to a parent, "I need $10." And if the parents learn to say, "No comprende. That kind of language doesn't work here. We've got plenty of money, but that's not how you get $10." Then you teach your teenager how to ask, "How can I earn $10?"

That is the magic of words. There is plenty of money here. There is money for everybody, but you just have to learn the magic words to get them. For everything you could possibly want. If you just learn the philosophy. How could I earn $10? Because you can't go to the soil and say, "Give me a harvest." You know the soil smiles and says, "Who is this clown that brings me his need and brings me no seed." And if you said to the soil, "I've got this seed and if I planted it, would you work while I sleep?" And the soil says, "No problem. Give me the seed. Go to sleep and I'll be working while you're sleeping."

If you just understand these simple principles, teaching them to a teenager (or adult) is sometimes just a matter of language. It's like an investment account instead of a savings account. Simple language, but so important. It is easy to stumble through almost a lifetime and not learn some of these simplicities. Then you have to put up with all the lack and all the challenges that don't work out simply from not reading the book, not listening to the tape, not sitting in the class, not studying your language and not being willing to search so you can then find.

But here is the great news. You can start this process anytime. For me it was at age 25. At 25 I'm broke. Six years later I'm a millionaire. Somebody says, "What kind of revolution, what kind of change, what kind of thinking, what kind of magic had to happen? Was it you?" And I say, "No. Any person, any six years,

36 to 42, 50 to 56. Whatever six years; whatever few years you go on an intensive, accelerated personal development curve, learning curve, application curve, and learning the disciplines. Now, it might not take the same amount of time, but I'm telling you the same changes and the same rewards in some different fashion are available for those who pay that six year price. And you might find that whether it's in the beginning to help get you started, or in the middle to keep you on track, that your language can have a great impact on your attitude, actions and results.

(by Jim Rohn)

1. Do you "believe the best, hope for the best, move toward the best"? What was your first reaction to that statement?

   _____
   _____
   _____

2. Jim uses the technique of creating positive "What if" questions to begin focusing his energy towards believing the best. Consider your long-range goals you set in previous chapter activities. What are the positive "what if" questions you are setting for yourself to achieve those goals?

   _____
   _____
   _____

3. When you were young, you may have been asked, "What are the magic words?" when you wanted something from family members or other adults. Jim talks about the "magic of words" and the effect language choice has on how well we succeed. He uses the example of calling a savings account an "investment account." Think of some examples in your daily language that you can change to make them "magic words" for you, creating a positive mindset of believing the best.

   _____
   _____
   _____

NEGOTIATING STEPS FOR SUCCESS

We use negotiating skills every day. They may be formal, recorded agreements or verbal or unspoken agreements with work colleagues, family, or friends. Making a purchase is a form of negotiation; we might sacrifice a particular product or service feature in exchange for another feature, quicker delivery, or a better price. In essence, negotiation is any event or situation that involves a trade or some form of giving and receiving.

Effective negotiators understand one basic concept: Good negotiations do not result in a "winner takes all" outcome. They consider all stakeholders and trade value equitably to achieve fair outcomes for all involved. In this activity, you will have a chance to evaluate your existing negotiation skills and formulate short-term goals for improving or strengthening your techniques.

For this activity, ask a friend or family member to be your negotiating partner. Decide on a common outcome, such as a dinner or another shared activity. Follow these steps through a negotiated process.

1. **Identify what you really need or want.** Each of you will state what is most important and why it is important to you. For example, you may want to go to a seafood restaurant rather than a pizza place because you had pizza for lunch.

2. **Differentiate between needs and wants and identify what you are willing to sacrifice.** As each of you considers what is critical to your position, think about what you might give up to meet the overall goal and whether the gain will be worth it. For example, you may be willing to go to an Italian restaurant because you could order something other than pizza.

3. **Build your case.** Take turns presenting facts that support your position. Consider the facts that will make the most difference to the person with whom you are negotiating, not just the ones that mean the most to you. How can you maximize the benefits for both of you? For example, you support your position of going to a seafood restaurant by pointing out that your negotiating partner loves the rolls that restaurant serves, and they have several dishes with seafood/pasta combinations.

4. **Prepare to defend your case.** Just as you have built a case in your mind for a position, your negotiating partner has done the same. Consider the potential arguments that might arise and think about how you might respond to them. Will your case stand up against these arguments?

5. **Identify and describe potential gains for each party.** Each of you has value you can offer and deliver. What will your negotiating partner gain

if you go with his/her position? How does that gain compare with yours if you choose your option? Is the trade equitable for both of you?

6. **Discuss and establish essential elements of the agreement.** Here is where you get to the details of your final agreement. You may pick and choose between your two positions to create balance. For example, you may agree to go for pizza tonight, but he/she agrees that the next time you go out it will be for seafood. You may compromise on an Italian restaurant that specializes in seafood/pasta dishes, or you may offer to pick up the tab if you both go for seafood tonight. These elements will come from what you are willing to sacrifice, the choices you made in building and defending your case, and the consideration of gains for each of you in the negotiation.

7. **Ensure outcomes are consistent with the terms of the agreement.** Will what you agreed to work for each of you? Do you need to make any adjustments so that both of you are satisfied with the outcome?

8. **Fulfill all oral and written commitments and promises.** Follow through with what you both agreed to, without disgruntled comments or reversal later on. Consider this: Do your actions consistently uphold your reputation as a fair and honorable person?

This negotiating sequence can be effective in any situation. Once you have practiced it a few times with family or friends, begin trying it out in work and other life situations. By following each of these steps consistently, you will find that your agreements will be satisfactory and successful for all parties involved.

COMMUNICATION GOALS

In Pillar Eight, you identified several individuals whom you wanted to talk with about your goals and how they might help you achieve them. In the chart below, list those whom you have talked with, the outcomes of those exchanges, and how you might increase your success with that person in the future by applying the listening or negotiation skills you learned in this chapter.

Whom I talked with about my goals	What happened when we talked and how they helped	Strategies for when I talk with this person again

Listed below are the Critical Skills needed to be proficient in this Pillar. Also listed are the Additional Essential Skills needed for mastery.

Critical Skills	Additional Essential Skills
Listening	Speaking
Observation	Optimism/Positive Attitude and Ambition
Respect	Accountability
Negotiation	Problem Solving

Pillar Eleven

"To lead others is to help them change their thoughts, beliefs, and actions for the better."

Before you begin this portion of the **Twelve Pillars Workbook**, read or reread Chapter 11, *The World Can Always Use One More Great Leader,* of **Twelve Pillars**.

Pillar Eleven

"The challenge of leadership is to be strong, but not rude; be kind, but not weak; be bold, but not a bully; be thoughtful, but not lazy; be humble, but not timid; be proud, but not arrogant; have humor, but without folly." (Charlie, ***Twelve Pillars****)*

Successful leadership begins with self-discipline and self-mastery. The most effective leaders are those who have chosen to develop the integrity, skills, knowledge, vision, attitude, and perspective required to inspire and encourage others.

In the home or at work, the effective leader understands and is fully committed to achieving the long-term vision for the family or company. This leader clearly communicates the guiding vision and its related mission, principles, and goals to those whose commitment and support are critical to fulfillment of the vision. He or she seeks to create and maintain an environment based on mutual respect and trust. The leader establishes and consistently models these standards from the outset.

At the core of an effective leader are honesty and integrity. To have integrity and to be honest requires a commitment to full-time practice in all circumstances. It also requires trust. Defined by *Webster's Dictionary* as "complete assurance and certitude regarding the character, ability, strength, or truth of someone or something," trust for leaders begins with an understanding of what each person expects from us. Failure to clarify specific expectations can set the stage for disappointment, failure, and loss of trust.

Honesty, integrity, optimism, vision, and trust are the foundations of successful relationships as well as successful leaders. The principles of leadership can apply to all aspects of our lives. As Charlie reminds Michael in **Twelve Pillars**, "Managers help people see themselves as they are. Leaders help people see themselves better than they are."

CRITICAL OUTCOMES FOR PILLAR ELEVEN:
- Identifying core leadership skills
- Recognizing leadership qualities in self and others

SEEKING MODELS OF LEADERSHIP

Leaders are all around you. As Charlie explained to Michael, "...anyone can be a great leader because all leadership means is that you have mastered the art of influencing others." Consider those in your workplace who are considered "leaders." Some have that title formally because they are managers, supervisors, or are in some other administrative position; others are considered "informal leaders." This second group descibes individuals who may not have the formal title, but are looked up to and respected for their leadership abilities regardless of their position in the organization. Consider who your work colleagues are most likely to listen to about work issues. Are there informal leaders in your workplace? How do your formal leaders regard those individuals? Wise leaders recognize and affirm leadership skills regardless of the organization's formal structure.

Just because an individual has the formal title of a leader, however, does not mean that he or she exhibits the characteristics you would want to model to be an effective leader. In the following activity, consider two individuals within your work setting who have formal leadership titles. Pick one who you feel demonstrates the kinds of leadership qualities you want to imitate, and one who may not be a good example of effective leadership. Compare them in the table on the next page.

LEADERSHIP COMPARISON IN YOUR ORGANIZATION

	Leader #1:	Leader #2:
Does this person seem to understand and be fully committed to your organization's vision? How does s/he demonstrate that?		
Has this leader encouraged and inspired others to share in this vision? If so, how? How do others respond to this person in his/her presence? In his/her absence?		
How well does this person meet commitments?		
What is his or her primary style or method of communication?		
How does this person promote trust, respect, collaboration, and unity in your workplace?		
What, if anything, have you learned about leadership by observing this individual?		

Are one or both of these individuals on your list of "Who I Want to Talk With" from Pillar Eight? Consider what you can learn from each of these individuals about how to achieve your long-term goals. One might act as inspiration and support, while the other might serve as a cautionary tale about how <u>not</u> to go about successfully reaching your goals.

MISTAKES TO AVOID

As you use this workbook, you will find activities that help you focus on developing those skills. You will also have opportunities to reflect on behaviors that may keep you from achieving the level of success for which you strive.

Which one of these **Mistakes to Avoid** is the one you need to work on changing in your life?

Skill: Leadership

- **Assuming a leadership role without the necessary skills.** Result: Lack of respect, few or no loyal followers, and unattained goals and objectives.

Skill: Trust

- **Violating the trust others invest in you.** Result: Break trust and you lose relationships, opportunities, and credibility.

Skill: Honesty/Integrity

- **Convincing yourself that lying is the better part of discretion.** Result: Confuse discretion with dishonesty. Cringe every time your lies come back to haunt you.

Skill: Optimism/Positive Attitude and Ambition

- **Using "be positive" to avoid dealing with or deflecting real problems.** Result: People will consider you ineffective in a team environment and won't consider you a real problem solving and decision making asset.

Skill: Speaking

- **Employing a condescending or patronizing manner.** Result: Nurture a growing desire in others to resent or shut you out.

Skill: Responsibility

- **Delegating tasks to individuals with unknown or questionable performance records.** Result: They will take you down with them. If you expect follow-through from people who have demonstrated repeatedly that they are incapable of following through, they will disappoint you time and again. You will begin to look like the incompetent one.

Skill: People Management

- **Insisting that others should know your expectations regardless of your ability to communicate them clearly.** Result: Expect to be frequently misunderstood. Be astounded by the varied and creative – if not appropriate – responses to your unspoken expectations. Find yourself pressed into the need to communicate more clearly when supervisors demand an explanation for the now legendary chaos, disorder, and poor productivity of your group.

SKILLS OF EXTRAORDINARY LEADERS

In the following article, Chris Widener (co-author of **Twelve Pillars**) offers ways to improve your leadership skills in daily life. Read the short narrative and then answer the reflective questions that follow.

What? You don't think that you are a leader? You are! Everyone influences others to some degree. Now, you may not be a very good leader... but that is altogether a different story! Even if you are in need of some help in the leadership department, and we all are, here are some skills you can work on immediately to help you become the leader you want to be. Then you can influence those around you like never before!

1. *__Good Communicator__. Extraordinary Leaders are those who can take the vision they have and communicate it in ways that their followers can easily understand, internalize, and own. Then, and only then, can they carry it out! So focus on speaking and writing more clearly, and with the passion that you have for the vision you have. Use different ways of communicating, including different ways verbally and non-verbally. Above all, communicate often!*

2. *__"Sees" the End Result Long Before Others__. I think the greatest compliment on my leadership skills I ever received came from a gentleman who told me that "you see things about 6 months before the rest of us." Without tooting my own horn (okay, a little bit maybe...), that is a skill of a leader. They are always looking out ahead of themselves and their situations. Followers are worried about what happens today, while leaders are thinking about and strategizing about what they see for tomorrow. Be constantly looking ahead. Practice making projections. Get good at "seeing" the future. When you can do this better than others, they will look to you for leadership!*

3. *__Ability to Define Goals for Self and Others__. Do you know what your goals are? Can you define them? Can you articulate them clearly (see number one)? Can you do this for those who follow? Can you define and set their goals? A Extraordinary Leader works at clarity and definition of goals so that they can be internalized and acted upon by others. Work hard at this skill and others will follow!*

4. *__Ability to Set Strategy and Course of Action__. What will you do to reach the goal? Many people can say where we should go, but it is the Extraordinary Leader who can lay out a plan for everyone to get there! Work at laying out a plan for you and your followers. Remember that there are people with different skill and passion levels, and take this into account! Get good at this and when people want to get to their goals in a hurry, they will call on you to lead!*

5. *__Ability to Teach Others__. One of the greatest leadership development companies in the world has been General Electric. This is because their CEO, Jack Welch, has always emphasized the need for current leaders to teach others. He himself spends what others would consider an extraordinary amount of time in the classroom teaching. But remember,*

he is an Extraordinary Leader and he is developing Extraordinary Leaders to follow behind him. Work hard at your teaching techniques, and be sure to use as many situations as possible for the opportunity to teach those who would follow.

6. **Ability to Inspire Others**. *You may have a great goal, but if you want to be an Extraordinary Leader, then you will have to put a little oomph under your followers! This is the ability to inspire! Work at helping them to see the big picture, the great end results, and how good it is going to be for them and others. Above all, make it exciting. If it is a good goal, it should be exciting. If it isn't exciting, then dump it and get a goal that others can get excited about! (See the next article, the MFS Classic, for more on inspiring others)*

7. **Delegates**. *An Extraordinary Leader is rarely a person who is doing everything him or herself. Extraordinary Leaders get their job done through others. They figure out the way, communicate the way, and inspire the followers to go that way, and then they get OUT OF THE WAY! Delegate to your people. Empower them! Set them free to soar! This is what an Extraordinary Leader does. Leaders who do it any other way are just extraordinarily tired at the end of the day with very little to show for it!*

(by Chris Widener)

1. Chris describes seven characteristics of Extraordinary Leaders. Begin your reflection on this article by rating yourself on where you are now with each of these characteristics on a scale of 1 (lowest) to 5 (highest):

    Good Communicator _____
    "Sees" the End Result Long Before Others _____
    Ability to Define Goals for Self and Others _____
    Ability to Set Strategy and Course of Action_____
    Ability to Teach Others _____
    Ability to Inspire Others _____
    Delegates _____

2. Choose the characteristic you rated the highest. Describe some of the ways you are being successful in this aspect of your life:

    _____
    _____
    _____
    _____

3. Now choose one of the characteristics you rated the lowest. What is one short-term goal you can set for yourself to improve this aspect of your leadership over the next two weeks?

_____

_____

_____

_____

4. In Pillar Six, you learned about the importance of role models and mentors in improving your skills and achieving your goals. Mentors are often examples of successful leaders. Reflect on the role models or mentors in your life who are successful leaders. What can you learn from them regarding the seven characteristics described in Chris's article?

_____

_____

_____

_____

_____

_____

_____

_____

_____

_____

LEADERS AS MODELS FOR SUCCESS

In the previous activity, you were asked to consider the leadership qualities and characteristics of people in your life who are leaders. As Charlie explained in **Twelve Pillars**, leaders can be anyone, not just people who lead nations, corporations, or social movements. This is not to say that great national or world leaders do not also have something to teach us about leadership.

In Pillar Seven, you learned the value of reading and may have included books or articles about individuals who were or are great leaders. If you did not, this is your opportunity to add to your Reading List and to consider how the lives of great leaders can provide an example for setting goals, defining vision, inspiring others, and teaching you about how you too can be a great leader.

1. Brainstorm a list of people you have read or heard about who are considered great leaders. List them in the spaces below:

    - _____
    - _____
    - _____
    - _____
    - _____
    - _____
    - _____
    - _____
    - _____
    - _____

2. Put an asterisk (*) next to the top two or three whom you really want to learn more about. If these individuals are currently living, begin your research by using an Internet search engine such as Google or Ask.com to find articles about their lives. Whether they are living or not, go to the library and ask the reference librarian for assistance in finding biographies or autobiographies about these individuals.

3. After you have done some preliminary searching and reading, choose one individual to spend more time learning about. Write the name of that leader in the space below, along with the reason you are most attracted to learning more about him or her.

   Leader: _____

   Why I chose this person:

   _____

4. Read and reflect on this individual's life. You may want to keep a journal or record your thoughts in the space below. Consider how this person reflected each of the characteristics of leadership. What can you learn from his or her life?

   _____

   _____

   _____

   _____

LEADERSHIP GOALS

Review your Goal statements from previous Pillars and identify the ones you feel will help strengthen your leadership skills in the space below. Include an action that you can take this week to bring you closer to those goals:

GOAL

ACTION

_____

_____

_____

_____

_____

_____

_____

_____

Listed below are the Critical Skills needed to be proficient in this Pillar. Also listed are the Additional Essential Skills needed for mastery.

Critical Skills	Additional Essential Skills
Leadership	Project Planning/Goal Setting
Trust	Listening
Honesty/Integrity	Responsibility
People Management	Team
Speaking	Social Interaction

Pillar Twelve

"Live a life that will help others spiritually, intellectually, physically, financially, and relationally. Live a life that serves as an example of what an exceptional life can look like."

Before you begin this portion of the **Twelve Pillars Workbook**, read or reread Chapter 12, *Leave a Legacy*, of **Twelve Pillars**.

Pillar Twelve

*"My legacy is fulfilled in part by teaching you how to live your best life. Your legacy will be to do the same for others. Give of yourself. Sacrifice for the good of others. Take the time to help others and to teach them. Be patient, loving, and loyal." (Charlie, **Twelve Pillars**)*

Leaving a legacy is not a one-time event. The legacies we leave behind will be a reflection of who we were on a consistent basis throughout our lives. Whether it's a sports figure or a person having made a significant contribution to society as a world leader or a servant of the greater good, historians describe people's contributions in the context of their character spanning a lifetime. One event may illuminate them, but it's the totality of their being: body, soul, and spirit. So too will it be for you. Each day matters, each human encounter matters and each skill matters.

As you take the gifts that Charlie has given you and Michael throughout the book **Twelve Pillars**, remember that your legacy begins with giving away what has been given to you – teach others what you have learned, practiced, and mastered. Our responsibility as leaders is to always demonstrate by our actions and words the very essence of who we want to be and who we know we will become.

Within our daily occupations, our chosen avocations, and our personal relationships, we encounter many opportunities to serve others. Whether this service is direct or indirect, public or private, compulsory or voluntary, we alone determine the character of our service. Poor, grudging service often leads to undesirable outcomes. Excellent, willing service usually leads to rich rewards, both tangible and intangible.

Dedicated service to our family members, friends, and community brings a special type of compensation. Whether performing necessary household tasks, helping a family member, assisting a friend or neighbor, or volunteering in a school or nursing home, we contribute our time and energy to help others. In return, we might receive a smile, a hug, a word of thanks, or just the knowledge that we have made a difference. These lasting treasures will improve our self-worth and our worth to others.

CRITICAL OUTCOMES FOR PILLAR TWELVE:
- Recognizing the impact one has on others.
- Determining a personal legacy for others.

YOUR LEGACY LETTER

In **Twelve Pillars**, Michael discovers that Charlie has not only served as his guide in his life-changing journey, but is the source of the Twelve Pillars he has been learning about. In his final role as a mentor, Charlie writes a letter to Michael that charges him to become a mentor, role model, and guide to others. By "passing the torch," Charlie teaches the final lesson of leaving a legacy for others to follow.

Reflect on the people in your life who are looking to you for guidance. It may be your children, a niece or nephew, family friends, work colleagues, neighbors, or others who see you as a role model for their lives. If you were to write a letter to leave for them as Charlie wrote for Michael, what would you say? What wisdom have you learned as you have worked through these activities and made changes in your own life?

In the space below and on the next page, begin drafting your letter to one of these special people in your life. Take time to edit and refine it and write a final version to send or give to this person. Make a difference in his or her life.

Dear _____,

_____
_____
_____
_____
_____
_____
_____
_____
_____

MISTAKES TO AVOID

As you use this workbook, you will find activities that help you focus on developing those skills. You will also have opportunities to reflect on behaviors that may keep you from achieving the level of success for which you strive.

Which one of these **Mistakes to Avoid** is the one you need to work on changing in your life?

Skill: Service to Others

- **Thinking more about your own needs while serving others.** Result: Your words may say, "How can I serve you?" but your attitude screams, "How can you serve me?"

- **Believing you are more important than those you serve.** Result: Act as if you are the most important person in the room and possibly end up being the only person in the room. Shout "Me, me, me!" and watch others flee, flee, flee!

- **Failing to listen with the intent to understand and assist.** Result: Assume you know what others want or need.

- **Adopting an arrogant attitude toward those you serve.** Result: Your motives will be questioned; trust and confidence in you will be fleeting.

Skill: Support Others

- **Seeking and accepting the continual support of others without offering or giving any in return.** Result: View life through self-centered glasses. Take until others can give no more.

- **Providing support only when it is convenient for you.** Result: Miss the deeper rewards that come from giving for the benefit of others.

- **Confusing the desire to control others with the desire to support them.** Result: Learn that those who simply require your support to regain stability will resent and dismiss your efforts to control them or their situation.

- **Telling someone what to do rather than making suggestions.** Result: You will be resented and your controlling ways rejected.

WHO MAKES A DIFFERENCE IN YOUR LIFE?

In the following article, Chris Widener (co-author of **Twelve Pillars**) considers those who make a difference in our lives. Read the short narrative and then answer the reflective questions which follow.

Take this quiz:

* *Name the three wealthiest people in the world.*
* *Name the last ten Heisman trophy winners.*
* *Name the last five winners of the Miss America contest.*
* *Name five people who have won the Nobel or Pulitzer Prize.*
* *How about the last five Academy Award winners for best picture.*

How did you do?

The point is, none of us remember the headliners of yesterday. These are no second-rate achievers. They are the best in their fields. But the applause dies, awards tarnish, achievements are forgotten, accolades and certificates are buried with their owners.

Here's another quiz. See how you do on this one:

* *Think of three people you enjoy spending time with.*
* *Name ten people who have taught you something worthwhile.*
* *Name five friends who have helped you in a difficult time.*
* *List five teachers who have aided your journey through school.*
* *Name five people whose stories have inspired you.*

Easier? The lesson? The people who make a difference in your life are not the ones with the credentials, but the ones that care.

(by Chris Widener)

Take Chris's quiz and answer the following:

- Name three people you enjoy spending time with:

    1. _____
    2. _____
    3. _____

- Name ten people who have taught you something worthwhile:

    1. _____
    2. _____
    3. _____
    4. _____
    5. _____
    6. _____
    7. _____
    8. _____
    9. _____
    10. _____

- Name five friends who have helped you in a difficult time:

    1. _____
    2. _____
    3. _____
    4. _____
    5. _____

- List five teachers who have aided your journey through school:

    1. _____
    2. _____
    3. _____
    4. _____
    5. _____

- Name five people whose stories have inspired you:

  1. _____
  2. _____
  3. _____
  4. _____
  5. _____

How many of these people know about your dreams and goals?

CHECKING IN ON YOUR GOALS

Throughout this workbook you have been asked to identify long-range and short-term goals. Rather than write more in this chapter, take time now to go back through each of the activities in the eleven previous chapters and reflect on what you have learned. Consider the following questions as you review your work:

- Have I followed through on all my commitments, goals, and plans?
- Would I change anything now that I have done more thinking and learning about myself?
- Which activities were especially hard for me? How did those exercises help me grow?
- Are there any lessons I have learned that I want to share with others?

Once you have reviewed and reflected on your past work, consider your next steps and answer the following questions:

- What strengths and weaknesses do I work on next for personal development?

  _____

- What changes do I need to make in Body, Soul, and Spirit?

  _____

- Which relationships most need tending in my life right now?

  _____

- How many goals on my list of "100 Things to Do Before I Die" can I now cross off? Which one will be next?

  _____

- What was my Best Opportunity today? Did I take advantage of it?

  _____

- Whom did I spend time with today? Were the associations positive ones?

  _____

- Name one book, article, or magazine you read this week that made a difference in how you think.
  _____

- Name one person with whom you talked about your goals and plans in the past week. (If there wasn't anyone, name two people you will talk with in the next week).
  _____

- Do you know exactly what you spent your money on today?
  _____

- How did you practice your listening skills this week?
  _____

- Name an effective leader you either watched or read about this week.
  _____

- Who is inspired by you?
  _____

"Let others lead small lives, but not you. Let others argue over small things, but not you. Let others cry over small hurts, but not you. Let others leave their future in someone else's hand, but not you."

—Charlie

For More Information

Forward ▶ Books

To order more books go to:
www.forwardbooks.com

To contact Forward Books by mail write to
Forward Books
15100 SE 38th St., #787
Bellevue WA, 98006

Other Titles available on www.forwardbooks.com:

"Living Well, Working Smart"
By Sue Mackey & Laura Tonkin

"The Honey-Do Survival Guide"

By Sue Mackey & Laura Tonkin

For more information on Sue Mackey and Laura Tonkin please visit
www.mackeygroup.com

Twelve Pillars of Success Workbook
The Skills You Need to Succeed

To order additional copies of **Twelve Pillars of Success Workbook**
by Sue Mackey and Laura Tonkin (Retail $12.95)
- 1 – 9 $9.00 ea.
- 10 – 24 $7.50 ea.
- 25 – 99 $6.00 ea.
- 100+ $5.00 ea

Washington residents please add 8.8% sales tax

To order copies of **Twelve Pillars**
by Jim Rohn and Chris Widener (Retail $12.95)
- 1 – 9 $9.00 ea.
- 10 – 24 $7.50 ea.
- 25 – 99 $6.00 ea.
- 100+ $5.00 ea.

Washington residents please add 8.8% sales tax

To order copies of **Living Well, Working Smart: Soft Skills for Success**
by Sue Mackey and Laura Tonkin (Retail $17.95)
- 1 – 9 $14.00 ea.
- 10 – 24 $12.50 ea.
- 25 – 99 $11.00 ea.
- 100+ $10.00 ea.

Washington residents please add 8.8% sales tax

To order copies of **The Honey-Do Survival Guide**
by Sue Mackey and Laura Tonkin (Retail $15.00)
- 1 – 9 $11.00 ea.
- 10 – 24 $ 9.50 ea.
- 25 – 99 $ 8.00 ea.
- 100+ $ 7.00 ea.

Washington residents please add 8.8% sales tax

Phone Orders:
425-466-6743

Visit us on the Web:
www.forwardbooks.com

Mail Orders:
Forward Books
15100 SE 38th St., #787
Bellevue, WA 98006

Books also available through
Jim Rohn International
www.jimrohn.com

Shipping & Handling

For Orders	Please Add
Up to $24.99	$4.95
$25 to $74.99	$5.95
$75 to $149.99	$6.95
$150 to $299.99	$8.95
$300 and Over	3%

Applies to US orders sent UPS Ground. Call for quotes on International and overnight shipping.